The Symptoms...

Auto-Immune disease is a roller coaster ride for those dealing with it. There are so many highs and lows that are faced on a daily basis. Symptoms come and go and only to come back again. It can be a battle to keep up with all the symptoms. This journal will help you keep track of the many symptoms and moments that can often be unpredictable. This journal is dedicated to all the auto immune warriors who face each day with bravery and strength the world has no clue. I see you all and have you in my heart as my fellow sisters and brothers.

-Rochelle Randall

Medications List:

Symptom Log

Description	MILD	MOD	SEVERE
--]	◯	◯	◯
--]	◯	◯	◯
--]	◯	◯	◯
--]	◯	◯	◯
--]	◯	◯	◯
--]	◯	◯	◯
--]	◯	◯	◯
--]	◯	◯	◯
--]	◯	◯	◯
--]	◯	◯	◯
--]	◯	◯	◯

NOTES:

Symptom Log

Description   MILD   MOD   SEVERE

--------------------------------------]   ◯   ◯   ◯

--------------------------------------]   ◯   ◯   ◯

--------------------------------------]   ◯   ◯   ◯

--------------------------------------]   ◯   ◯   ◯

--------------------------------------]   ◯   ◯   ◯

--------------------------------------]   ◯   ◯   ◯

--------------------------------------]   ◯   ◯   ◯

--------------------------------------]   ◯   ◯   ◯

--------------------------------------]   ◯   ◯   ◯

--------------------------------------]   ◯   ◯   ◯

--------------------------------------]   ◯   ◯   ◯

NOTES:

Symptom Log

Description	MILD	MOD	SEVERE
----------------------------------]	◯	◯	◯
----------------------------------]	◯	◯	◯
----------------------------------]	◯	◯	◯
----------------------------------]	◯	◯	◯
----------------------------------]	◯	◯	◯
----------------------------------]	◯	◯	◯
----------------------------------]	◯	◯	◯
----------------------------------]	◯	◯	◯
----------------------------------]	◯	◯	◯
----------------------------------]	◯	◯	◯
----------------------------------]	◯	◯	◯

NOTES:

Symptom Log

Description   MILD   MOD   SEVERE

Description	MILD	MOD	SEVERE
-------------------------------------]	◯	◯	◯
-------------------------------------]	◯	◯	◯
-------------------------------------]	◯	◯	◯
-------------------------------------]	◯	◯	◯
-------------------------------------]	◯	◯	◯
-------------------------------------]	◯	◯	◯
-------------------------------------]	◯	◯	◯
-------------------------------------]	◯	◯	◯
-------------------------------------]	◯	◯	◯
-------------------------------------]	◯	◯	◯
-------------------------------------]	◯	◯	◯

NOTES:

Symptom Log

Description	MILD	MOD	SEVERE

--------------------------------] ○ ○ ○

--------------------------------] ○ ○ ○

--------------------------------] ○ ○ ○

--------------------------------] ○ ○ ○

--------------------------------] ○ ○ ○

--------------------------------] ○ ○ ○

--------------------------------] ○ ○ ○

--------------------------------] ○ ○ ○

--------------------------------] ○ ○ ○

--------------------------------] ○ ○ ○

--------------------------------] ○ ○ ○

NOTES:

Symptom Log

Description   MILD   MOD   SEVERE

------------------------------------]   ◯   ◯   ◯

------------------------------------]   ◯   ◯   ◯

------------------------------------]   ◯   ◯   ◯

------------------------------------]   ◯   ◯   ◯

------------------------------------]   ◯   ◯   ◯

------------------------------------]   ◯   ◯   ◯

------------------------------------]   ◯   ◯   ◯

------------------------------------]   ◯   ◯   ◯

------------------------------------]   ◯   ◯   ◯

------------------------------------]   ◯   ◯   ◯

------------------------------------]   ◯   ◯   ◯

NOTES:

Symptom Log

Description	MILD	MOD	SEVERE
---]	◯	◯	◯
---]	◯	◯	◯
---]	◯	◯	◯
---]	◯	◯	◯
---]	◯	◯	◯
---]	◯	◯	◯
---]	◯	◯	◯
---]	◯	◯	◯
---]	◯	◯	◯
---]	◯	◯	◯
---]	◯	◯	◯

NOTES:

Symptom Log

Description	MILD	MOD	SEVERE
----------------------------------]	◯	◯	◯
----------------------------------]	◯	◯	◯
----------------------------------]	◯	◯	◯
----------------------------------]	◯	◯	◯
----------------------------------]	◯	◯	◯
----------------------------------]	◯	◯	◯
----------------------------------]	◯	◯	◯
----------------------------------]	◯	◯	◯
----------------------------------]	◯	◯	◯
----------------------------------]	◯	◯	◯
----------------------------------]	◯	◯	◯

NOTES:

Symptom Log

Description	MILD	MOD	SEVERE
------------------------------------]	◯	◯	◯
------------------------------------]	◯	◯	◯
------------------------------------]	◯	◯	◯
------------------------------------]	◯	◯	◯
------------------------------------]	◯	◯	◯
------------------------------------]	◯	◯	◯
------------------------------------]	◯	◯	◯
------------------------------------]	◯	◯	◯
------------------------------------]	◯	◯	◯
------------------------------------]	◯	◯	◯
------------------------------------]	◯	◯	◯

NOTES:

Symptom Log

Description   MILD   MOD   SEVERE

-------------------------------------]   ◯   ◯   ◯

-------------------------------------]   ◯   ◯   ◯

-------------------------------------]   ◯   ◯   ◯

-------------------------------------]   ◯   ◯   ◯

-------------------------------------]   ◯   ◯   ◯

-------------------------------------]   ◯   ◯   ◯

-------------------------------------]   ◯   ◯   ◯

-------------------------------------]   ◯   ◯   ◯

-------------------------------------]   ◯   ◯   ◯

-------------------------------------]   ◯   ◯   ◯

-------------------------------------]   ◯   ◯   ◯

NOTES:

Symptom Log

Description	MILD	MOD	SEVERE
-----------------------------]	◯	◯	◯
-----------------------------]	◯	◯	◯
-----------------------------]	◯	◯	◯
-----------------------------]	◯	◯	◯
-----------------------------]	◯	◯	◯
-----------------------------]	◯	◯	◯
-----------------------------]	◯	◯	◯
-----------------------------]	◯	◯	◯
-----------------------------]	◯	◯	◯
-----------------------------]	◯	◯	◯
-----------------------------]	◯	◯	◯

NOTES:

Symptom Log

Description   MILD   MOD   SEVERE

-------------------------------------] ◯ ◯ ◯

-------------------------------------] ◯ ◯ ◯

-------------------------------------] ◯ ◯ ◯

-------------------------------------] ◯ ◯ ◯

-------------------------------------] ◯ ◯ ◯

-------------------------------------] ◯ ◯ ◯

-------------------------------------] ◯ ◯ ◯

-------------------------------------] ◯ ◯ ◯

-------------------------------------] ◯ ◯ ◯

-------------------------------------] ◯ ◯ ◯

-------------------------------------] ◯ ◯ ◯

NOTES:

Symptom Log

Description	MILD	MOD	SEVERE
--------------------------------]	◯	◯	◯
--------------------------------]	◯	◯	◯
--------------------------------]	◯	◯	◯
--------------------------------]	◯	◯	◯
--------------------------------]	◯	◯	◯
--------------------------------]	◯	◯	◯
--------------------------------]	◯	◯	◯
--------------------------------]	◯	◯	◯
--------------------------------]	◯	◯	◯
--------------------------------]	◯	◯	◯
--------------------------------]	◯	◯	◯

NOTES:

Symptom Log

Description   MILD   MOD   SEVERE

-----------------------------------]   ◯   ◯   ◯

-----------------------------------]   ◯   ◯   ◯

-----------------------------------]   ◯   ◯   ◯

-----------------------------------]   ◯   ◯   ◯

-----------------------------------]   ◯   ◯   ◯

-----------------------------------]   ◯   ◯   ◯

-----------------------------------]   ◯   ◯   ◯

-----------------------------------]   ◯   ◯   ◯

-----------------------------------]   ◯   ◯   ◯

-----------------------------------]   ◯   ◯   ◯

-----------------------------------]   ◯   ◯   ◯

NOTES:

Symptom Log

Description	MILD	MOD	SEVERE
-----------------------------------]	○	○	○
-----------------------------------]	○	○	○
-----------------------------------]	○	○	○
-----------------------------------]	○	○	○
-----------------------------------]	○	○	○
-----------------------------------]	○	○	○
-----------------------------------]	○	○	○
-----------------------------------]	○	○	○
-----------------------------------]	○	○	○
-----------------------------------]	○	○	○
-----------------------------------]	○	○	○

NOTES:

Symptom Log

Description	MILD	MOD	SEVERE
----------------------------------]	◯	◯	◯
----------------------------------]	◯	◯	◯
----------------------------------]	◯	◯	◯
----------------------------------]	◯	◯	◯
----------------------------------]	◯	◯	◯
----------------------------------]	◯	◯	◯
----------------------------------]	◯	◯	◯
----------------------------------]	◯	◯	◯
----------------------------------]	◯	◯	◯
----------------------------------]	◯	◯	◯
----------------------------------]	◯	◯	◯

NOTES:

Symptom Log

Description	MILD	MOD	SEVERE
---------------------------]	◯	◯	◯
---------------------------]	◯	◯	◯
---------------------------]	◯	◯	◯
---------------------------]	◯	◯	◯
---------------------------]	◯	◯	◯
---------------------------]	◯	◯	◯
---------------------------]	◯	◯	◯
---------------------------]	◯	◯	◯
---------------------------]	◯	◯	◯
---------------------------]	◯	◯	◯
---------------------------]	◯	◯	◯

NOTES:

Symptom Log

Description   MILD   MOD   SEVERE

-----------------------------------] ◯ ◯ ◯

-----------------------------------] ◯ ◯ ◯

-----------------------------------] ◯ ◯ ◯

-----------------------------------] ◯ ◯ ◯

-----------------------------------] ◯ ◯ ◯

-----------------------------------] ◯ ◯ ◯

-----------------------------------] ◯ ◯ ◯

-----------------------------------] ◯ ◯ ◯

-----------------------------------] ◯ ◯ ◯

-----------------------------------] ◯ ◯ ◯

-----------------------------------] ◯ ◯ ◯

NOTES:

Symptom Log

Description	MILD	MOD	SEVERE
------------------------------]	◯	◯	◯
------------------------------]	◯	◯	◯
------------------------------]	◯	◯	◯
------------------------------]	◯	◯	◯
------------------------------]	◯	◯	◯
------------------------------]	◯	◯	◯
------------------------------]	◯	◯	◯
------------------------------]	◯	◯	◯
------------------------------]	◯	◯	◯
------------------------------]	◯	◯	◯
------------------------------]	◯	◯	◯

NOTES:

Symptom Log

Description	MILD	MOD	SEVERE
--------------------------------]	○	○	○
--------------------------------]	○	○	○
--------------------------------]	○	○	○
--------------------------------]	○	○	○
--------------------------------]	○	○	○
--------------------------------]	○	○	○
--------------------------------]	○	○	○
--------------------------------]	○	○	○
--------------------------------]	○	○	○
--------------------------------]	○	○	○
--------------------------------]	○	○	○

NOTES:

Symptom Log

Description	MILD	MOD	SEVERE
------------------------------------]	◯	◯	◯
------------------------------------]	◯	◯	◯
------------------------------------]	◯	◯	◯
------------------------------------]	◯	◯	◯
------------------------------------]	◯	◯	◯
------------------------------------]	◯	◯	◯
------------------------------------]	◯	◯	◯
------------------------------------]	◯	◯	◯
------------------------------------]	◯	◯	◯
------------------------------------]	◯	◯	◯
------------------------------------]	◯	◯	◯

NOTES:

Symptom Log

Description   MILD   MOD   SEVERE

-----------------------------------] ◯ ◯ ◯

-----------------------------------] ◯ ◯ ◯

-----------------------------------] ◯ ◯ ◯

-----------------------------------] ◯ ◯ ◯

-----------------------------------] ◯ ◯ ◯

-----------------------------------] ◯ ◯ ◯

-----------------------------------] ◯ ◯ ◯

-----------------------------------] ◯ ◯ ◯

-----------------------------------] ◯ ◯ ◯

-----------------------------------] ◯ ◯ ◯

-----------------------------------] ◯ ◯ ◯

NOTES:

Symptom Log

Description	MILD	MOD	SEVERE
------------------------------------]	◯	◯	◯
------------------------------------]	◯	◯	◯
------------------------------------]	◯	◯	◯
------------------------------------]	◯	◯	◯
------------------------------------]	◯	◯	◯
------------------------------------]	◯	◯	◯
------------------------------------]	◯	◯	◯
------------------------------------]	◯	◯	◯
------------------------------------]	◯	◯	◯
------------------------------------]	◯	◯	◯
------------------------------------]	◯	◯	◯

NOTES:

Symptom Log

Description	MILD	MOD	SEVERE
----------------------------------]	◯	◯	◯
----------------------------------]	◯	◯	◯
----------------------------------]	◯	◯	◯
----------------------------------]	◯	◯	◯
----------------------------------]	◯	◯	◯
----------------------------------]	◯	◯	◯
----------------------------------]	◯	◯	◯
----------------------------------]	◯	◯	◯
----------------------------------]	◯	◯	◯
----------------------------------]	◯	◯	◯
----------------------------------]	◯	◯	◯

NOTES:

Symptom Log

Description	MILD	MOD	SEVERE
--------------------------------]	◯	◯	◯
--------------------------------]	◯	◯	◯
--------------------------------]	◯	◯	◯
--------------------------------]	◯	◯	◯
--------------------------------]	◯	◯	◯
--------------------------------]	◯	◯	◯
--------------------------------]	◯	◯	◯
--------------------------------]	◯	◯	◯
--------------------------------]	◯	◯	◯
--------------------------------]	◯	◯	◯
--------------------------------]	◯	◯	◯

NOTES:

Symptom Log

Description   MILD   MOD   SEVERE

-----------------------------------]   ◯   ◯   ◯

-----------------------------------]   ◯   ◯   ◯

-----------------------------------]   ◯   ◯   ◯

-----------------------------------]   ◯   ◯   ◯

-----------------------------------]   ◯   ◯   ◯

-----------------------------------]   ◯   ◯   ◯

-----------------------------------]   ◯   ◯   ◯

-----------------------------------]   ◯   ◯   ◯

-----------------------------------]   ◯   ◯   ◯

-----------------------------------]   ◯   ◯   ◯

-----------------------------------]   ◯   ◯   ◯

NOTES:

Symptom Log

Description	MILD	MOD	SEVERE
--]	◯	◯	◯
--]	◯	◯	◯
--]	◯	◯	◯
--]	◯	◯	◯
--]	◯	◯	◯
--]	◯	◯	◯
--]	◯	◯	◯
--]	◯	◯	◯
--]	◯	◯	◯
--]	◯	◯	◯
--]	◯	◯	◯

NOTES:

Symptom Log

Description   MILD   MOD   SEVERE

-----------------------------------] ◯   ◯   ◯

-----------------------------------] ◯   ◯   ◯

-----------------------------------] ◯   ◯   ◯

-----------------------------------] ◯   ◯   ◯

-----------------------------------] ◯   ◯   ◯

-----------------------------------] ◯   ◯   ◯

-----------------------------------] ◯   ◯   ◯

-----------------------------------] ◯   ◯   ◯

-----------------------------------] ◯   ◯   ◯

-----------------------------------] ◯   ◯   ◯

-----------------------------------] ◯   ◯   ◯

NOTES:

Symptom Log

Description	MILD	MOD	SEVERE
------------------------------------]	O	O	O
------------------------------------]	O	O	O
------------------------------------]	O	O	O
------------------------------------]	O	O	O
------------------------------------]	O	O	O
------------------------------------]	O	O	O
------------------------------------]	O	O	O
------------------------------------]	O	O	O
------------------------------------]	O	O	O
------------------------------------]	O	O	O
------------------------------------]	O	O	O

NOTES:

Symptom Log

Description   MILD   MOD   SEVERE

------------------------------------] ◯ ◯ ◯

------------------------------------] ◯ ◯ ◯

------------------------------------] ◯ ◯ ◯

------------------------------------] ◯ ◯ ◯

------------------------------------] ◯ ◯ ◯

------------------------------------] ◯ ◯ ◯

------------------------------------] ◯ ◯ ◯

------------------------------------] ◯ ◯ ◯

------------------------------------] ◯ ◯ ◯

------------------------------------] ◯ ◯ ◯

------------------------------------] ◯ ◯ ◯

NOTES:

Symptom Log

Description	MILD	MOD	SEVERE
--------------------------------]	○	○	○
--------------------------------]	○	○	○
--------------------------------]	○	○	○
--------------------------------]	○	○	○
--------------------------------]	○	○	○
--------------------------------]	○	○	○
--------------------------------]	○	○	○
--------------------------------]	○	○	○
--------------------------------]	○	○	○
--------------------------------]	○	○	○
--------------------------------]	○	○	○

NOTES:

Symptom Log

Description   MILD   MOD   SEVERE

-------------------------------------] ◯ ◯ ◯

-------------------------------------] ◯ ◯ ◯

-------------------------------------] ◯ ◯ ◯

-------------------------------------] ◯ ◯ ◯

-------------------------------------] ◯ ◯ ◯

-------------------------------------] ◯ ◯ ◯

-------------------------------------] ◯ ◯ ◯

-------------------------------------] ◯ ◯ ◯

-------------------------------------] ◯ ◯ ◯

-------------------------------------] ◯ ◯ ◯

-------------------------------------] ◯ ◯ ◯

NOTES:

Symptom Log

Description	MILD	MOD	SEVERE
-----------------------------------]	◯	◯	◯
-----------------------------------]	◯	◯	◯
-----------------------------------]	◯	◯	◯
-----------------------------------]	◯	◯	◯
-----------------------------------]	◯	◯	◯
-----------------------------------]	◯	◯	◯
-----------------------------------]	◯	◯	◯
-----------------------------------]	◯	◯	◯
-----------------------------------]	◯	◯	◯
-----------------------------------]	◯	◯	◯
-----------------------------------]	◯	◯	◯

NOTES:

Symptom Log

Description	MILD	MOD	SEVERE
-----------------------------------]	◯	◯	◯
-----------------------------------]	◯	◯	◯
-----------------------------------]	◯	◯	◯
-----------------------------------]	◯	◯	◯
-----------------------------------]	◯	◯	◯
-----------------------------------]	◯	◯	◯
-----------------------------------]	◯	◯	◯
-----------------------------------]	◯	◯	◯
-----------------------------------]	◯	◯	◯
-----------------------------------]	◯	◯	◯
-----------------------------------]	◯	◯	◯

NOTES:

Symptom Log

Description	MILD	MOD	SEVERE
------------------------------]	◯	◯	◯
------------------------------]	◯	◯	◯
------------------------------]	◯	◯	◯
------------------------------]	◯	◯	◯
------------------------------]	◯	◯	◯
------------------------------]	◯	◯	◯
------------------------------]	◯	◯	◯
------------------------------]	◯	◯	◯
------------------------------]	◯	◯	◯
------------------------------]	◯	◯	◯
------------------------------]	◯	◯	◯

NOTES:

Symptom Log

Description	MILD	MOD	SEVERE
-------------------------------------]	◯	◯	◯
-------------------------------------]	◯	◯	◯
-------------------------------------]	◯	◯	◯
-------------------------------------]	◯	◯	◯
-------------------------------------]	◯	◯	◯
-------------------------------------]	◯	◯	◯
-------------------------------------]	◯	◯	◯
-------------------------------------]	◯	◯	◯
-------------------------------------]	◯	◯	◯
-------------------------------------]	◯	◯	◯
-------------------------------------]	◯	◯	◯

NOTES:

Symptom Log

Description	MILD	MOD	SEVERE
------------------------------]	◯	◯	◯
------------------------------]	◯	◯	◯
------------------------------]	◯	◯	◯
------------------------------]	◯	◯	◯
------------------------------]	◯	◯	◯
------------------------------]	◯	◯	◯
------------------------------]	◯	◯	◯
------------------------------]	◯	◯	◯
------------------------------]	◯	◯	◯
------------------------------]	◯	◯	◯
------------------------------]	◯	◯	◯

NOTES:

Symptom Log

Description	MILD	MOD	SEVERE
----------------------------------]	◯	◯	◯
----------------------------------]	◯	◯	◯
----------------------------------]	◯	◯	◯
----------------------------------]	◯	◯	◯
----------------------------------]	◯	◯	◯
----------------------------------]	◯	◯	◯
----------------------------------]	◯	◯	◯
----------------------------------]	◯	◯	◯
----------------------------------]	◯	◯	◯
----------------------------------]	◯	◯	◯
----------------------------------]	◯	◯	◯

NOTES:

Symptom Log

Description	MILD	MOD	SEVERE
----------------------------------]	◯	◯	◯
----------------------------------]	◯	◯	◯
----------------------------------]	◯	◯	◯
----------------------------------]	◯	◯	◯
----------------------------------]	◯	◯	◯
----------------------------------]	◯	◯	◯
----------------------------------]	◯	◯	◯
----------------------------------]	◯	◯	◯
----------------------------------]	◯	◯	◯
----------------------------------]	◯	◯	◯
----------------------------------]	◯	◯	◯

NOTES:

Symptom Log

Description	MILD	MOD	SEVERE
--]	◯	◯	◯
--]	◯	◯	◯
--]	◯	◯	◯
--]	◯	◯	◯
--]	◯	◯	◯
--]	◯	◯	◯
--]	◯	◯	◯
--]	◯	◯	◯
--]	◯	◯	◯
--]	◯	◯	◯
--]	◯	◯	◯

NOTES:

Symptom Log

Description	MILD	MOD	SEVERE
--]	◯	◯	◯
--]	◯	◯	◯
--]	◯	◯	◯
--]	◯	◯	◯
--]	◯	◯	◯
--]	◯	◯	◯
--]	◯	◯	◯
--]	◯	◯	◯
--]	◯	◯	◯
--]	◯	◯	◯
--]	◯	◯	◯

NOTES:

Symptom Log

Description	MILD	MOD	SEVERE
---------------------------------]	◯	◯	◯
---------------------------------]	◯	◯	◯
---------------------------------]	◯	◯	◯
---------------------------------]	◯	◯	◯
---------------------------------]	◯	◯	◯
---------------------------------]	◯	◯	◯
---------------------------------]	◯	◯	◯
---------------------------------]	◯	◯	◯
---------------------------------]	◯	◯	◯
---------------------------------]	◯	◯	◯
---------------------------------]	◯	◯	◯

NOTES:

Symptom Log

Description	MILD	MOD	SEVERE
----------------------------------]	◯	◯	◯
----------------------------------]	◯	◯	◯
----------------------------------]	◯	◯	◯
----------------------------------]	◯	◯	◯
----------------------------------]	◯	◯	◯
----------------------------------]	◯	◯	◯
----------------------------------]	◯	◯	◯
----------------------------------]	◯	◯	◯
----------------------------------]	◯	◯	◯
----------------------------------]	◯	◯	◯
----------------------------------]	◯	◯	◯

NOTES:

Symptom Log

Description	MILD	MOD	SEVERE
-----------------------------------]	◯	◯	◯
-----------------------------------]	◯	◯	◯
-----------------------------------]	◯	◯	◯
-----------------------------------]	◯	◯	◯
-----------------------------------]	◯	◯	◯
-----------------------------------]	◯	◯	◯
-----------------------------------]	◯	◯	◯
-----------------------------------]	◯	◯	◯
-----------------------------------]	◯	◯	◯
-----------------------------------]	◯	◯	◯
-----------------------------------]	◯	◯	◯

NOTES:

Symptom Log

Description	MILD	MOD	SEVERE
----------------------------------]	◯	◯	◯
----------------------------------]	◯	◯	◯
----------------------------------]	◯	◯	◯
----------------------------------]	◯	◯	◯
----------------------------------]	◯	◯	◯
----------------------------------]	◯	◯	◯
----------------------------------]	◯	◯	◯
----------------------------------]	◯	◯	◯
----------------------------------]	◯	◯	◯
----------------------------------]	◯	◯	◯
----------------------------------]	◯	◯	◯

NOTES:

Symptom Log

Description	MILD	MOD	SEVERE
----------------------------------]	◯	◯	◯
----------------------------------]	◯	◯	◯
----------------------------------]	◯	◯	◯
----------------------------------]	◯	◯	◯
----------------------------------]	◯	◯	◯
----------------------------------]	◯	◯	◯
----------------------------------]	◯	◯	◯
----------------------------------]	◯	◯	◯
----------------------------------]	◯	◯	◯
----------------------------------]	◯	◯	◯
----------------------------------]	◯	◯	◯

NOTES:

Symptom Log

Description	MILD	MOD	SEVERE
------------------------------]	◯	◯	◯
------------------------------]	◯	◯	◯
------------------------------]	◯	◯	◯
------------------------------]	◯	◯	◯
------------------------------]	◯	◯	◯
------------------------------]	◯	◯	◯
------------------------------]	◯	◯	◯
------------------------------]	◯	◯	◯
------------------------------]	◯	◯	◯
------------------------------]	◯	◯	◯
------------------------------]	◯	◯	◯

NOTES:

Symptom Log

Description	MILD	MOD	SEVERE
----------------------------------]	○	○	○
----------------------------------]	○	○	○
----------------------------------]	○	○	○
----------------------------------]	○	○	○
----------------------------------]	○	○	○
----------------------------------]	○	○	○
----------------------------------]	○	○	○
----------------------------------]	○	○	○
----------------------------------]	○	○	○
----------------------------------]	○	○	○
----------------------------------]	○	○	○

NOTES:

Symptom Log

Description	MILD	MOD	SEVERE
-----------------------------------]	◯	◯	◯
-----------------------------------]	◯	◯	◯
-----------------------------------]	◯	◯	◯
-----------------------------------]	◯	◯	◯
-----------------------------------]	◯	◯	◯
-----------------------------------]	◯	◯	◯
-----------------------------------]	◯	◯	◯
-----------------------------------]	◯	◯	◯
-----------------------------------]	◯	◯	◯
-----------------------------------]	◯	◯	◯
-----------------------------------]	◯	◯	◯

NOTES:

Symptom Log

Description   MILD   MOD   SEVERE

------------------------------------]   ◯   ◯   ◯

------------------------------------]   ◯   ◯   ◯

------------------------------------]   ◯   ◯   ◯

------------------------------------]   ◯   ◯   ◯

------------------------------------]   ◯   ◯   ◯

------------------------------------]   ◯   ◯   ◯

------------------------------------]   ◯   ◯   ◯

------------------------------------]   ◯   ◯   ◯

------------------------------------]   ◯   ◯   ◯

------------------------------------]   ◯   ◯   ◯

------------------------------------]   ◯   ◯   ◯

NOTES:

Symptom Log

Description	MILD	MOD	SEVERE
-------------------------------]	○	○	○
-------------------------------]	○	○	○
-------------------------------]	○	○	○
-------------------------------]	○	○	○
-------------------------------]	○	○	○
-------------------------------]	○	○	○
-------------------------------]	○	○	○
-------------------------------]	○	○	○
-------------------------------]	○	○	○
-------------------------------]	○	○	○
-------------------------------]	○	○	○

NOTES:

Symptom Log

Description	MILD	MOD	SEVERE
-----------------------------------]	○	○	○
-----------------------------------]	○	○	○
-----------------------------------]	○	○	○
-----------------------------------]	○	○	○
-----------------------------------]	○	○	○
-----------------------------------]	○	○	○
-----------------------------------]	○	○	○
-----------------------------------]	○	○	○
-----------------------------------]	○	○	○
-----------------------------------]	○	○	○
-----------------------------------]	○	○	○

NOTES:

Symptom Log

Description	MILD	MOD	SEVERE
----------------------------------]	◯	◯	◯
----------------------------------]	◯	◯	◯
----------------------------------]	◯	◯	◯
----------------------------------]	◯	◯	◯
----------------------------------]	◯	◯	◯
----------------------------------]	◯	◯	◯
----------------------------------]	◯	◯	◯
----------------------------------]	◯	◯	◯
----------------------------------]	◯	◯	◯
----------------------------------]	◯	◯	◯
----------------------------------]	◯	◯	◯

NOTES:

Symptom Log

Description	MILD	MOD	SEVERE
------------------------------------]	◯	◯	◯
------------------------------------]	◯	◯	◯
------------------------------------]	◯	◯	◯
------------------------------------]	◯	◯	◯
------------------------------------]	◯	◯	◯
------------------------------------]	◯	◯	◯
------------------------------------]	◯	◯	◯
------------------------------------]	◯	◯	◯
------------------------------------]	◯	◯	◯
------------------------------------]	◯	◯	◯
------------------------------------]	◯	◯	◯

NOTES:

Symptom Log

Description	MILD	MOD	SEVERE
----------------------------------]	◯	◯	◯
----------------------------------]	◯	◯	◯
----------------------------------]	◯	◯	◯
----------------------------------]	◯	◯	◯
----------------------------------]	◯	◯	◯
----------------------------------]	◯	◯	◯
----------------------------------]	◯	◯	◯
----------------------------------]	◯	◯	◯
----------------------------------]	◯	◯	◯
----------------------------------]	◯	◯	◯
----------------------------------]	◯	◯	◯

NOTES:

Symptom Log

Description   MILD   MOD   SEVERE

-------------------------------] ◯ ◯ ◯

-------------------------------] ◯ ◯ ◯

-------------------------------] ◯ ◯ ◯

-------------------------------] ◯ ◯ ◯

-------------------------------] ◯ ◯ ◯

-------------------------------] ◯ ◯ ◯

-------------------------------] ◯ ◯ ◯

-------------------------------] ◯ ◯ ◯

-------------------------------] ◯ ◯ ◯

-------------------------------] ◯ ◯ ◯

-------------------------------] ◯ ◯ ◯

NOTES:

Symptom Log

Description	MILD	MOD	SEVERE
-------------------------------]	◯	◯	◯
-------------------------------]	◯	◯	◯
-------------------------------]	◯	◯	◯
-------------------------------]	◯	◯	◯
-------------------------------]	◯	◯	◯
-------------------------------]	◯	◯	◯
-------------------------------]	◯	◯	◯
-------------------------------]	◯	◯	◯
-------------------------------]	◯	◯	◯
-------------------------------]	◯	◯	◯
-------------------------------]	◯	◯	◯

NOTES:

Symptom Log

Description	MILD	MOD	SEVERE
----------------------------------]	◯	◯	◯
----------------------------------]	◯	◯	◯
----------------------------------]	◯	◯	◯
----------------------------------]	◯	◯	◯
----------------------------------]	◯	◯	◯
----------------------------------]	◯	◯	◯
----------------------------------]	◯	◯	◯
----------------------------------]	◯	◯	◯
----------------------------------]	◯	◯	◯
----------------------------------]	◯	◯	◯
----------------------------------]	◯	◯	◯

NOTES:

Symptom Log

Description	MILD	MOD	SEVERE
----------------------------------]	◯	◯	◯
----------------------------------]	◯	◯	◯
----------------------------------]	◯	◯	◯
----------------------------------]	◯	◯	◯
----------------------------------]	◯	◯	◯
----------------------------------]	◯	◯	◯
----------------------------------]	◯	◯	◯
----------------------------------]	◯	◯	◯
----------------------------------]	◯	◯	◯
----------------------------------]	◯	◯	◯
----------------------------------]	◯	◯	◯

NOTES:

Symptom Log

Description	MILD	MOD	SEVERE
--------------------------------]	○	○	○
--------------------------------]	○	○	○
--------------------------------]	○	○	○
--------------------------------]	○	○	○
--------------------------------]	○	○	○
--------------------------------]	○	○	○
--------------------------------]	○	○	○
--------------------------------]	○	○	○
--------------------------------]	○	○	○
--------------------------------]	○	○	○
--------------------------------]	○	○	○

NOTES:

Symptom Log

Description	MILD	MOD	SEVERE
------------------------------]	◯	◯	◯
------------------------------]	◯	◯	◯
------------------------------]	◯	◯	◯
------------------------------]	◯	◯	◯
------------------------------]	◯	◯	◯
------------------------------]	◯	◯	◯
------------------------------]	◯	◯	◯
------------------------------]	◯	◯	◯
------------------------------]	◯	◯	◯
------------------------------]	◯	◯	◯
------------------------------]	◯	◯	◯

NOTES:

Symptom Log

Description	MILD	MOD	SEVERE
----------------------------------]	◯	◯	◯
----------------------------------]	◯	◯	◯
----------------------------------]	◯	◯	◯
----------------------------------]	◯	◯	◯
----------------------------------]	◯	◯	◯
----------------------------------]	◯	◯	◯
----------------------------------]	◯	◯	◯
----------------------------------]	◯	◯	◯
----------------------------------]	◯	◯	◯
----------------------------------]	◯	◯	◯
----------------------------------]	◯	◯	◯

NOTES:

Symptom Log

Description   MILD   MOD   SEVERE

----------------------------------]   ◯   ◯   ◯

----------------------------------]   ◯   ◯   ◯

----------------------------------]   ◯   ◯   ◯

----------------------------------]   ◯   ◯   ◯

----------------------------------]   ◯   ◯   ◯

----------------------------------]   ◯   ◯   ◯

----------------------------------]   ◯   ◯   ◯

----------------------------------]   ◯   ◯   ◯

----------------------------------]   ◯   ◯   ◯

----------------------------------]   ◯   ◯   ◯

----------------------------------]   ◯   ◯   ◯

NOTES:

Symptom Log

Description	MILD	MOD	SEVERE
------------------------------------]	◯	◯	◯
------------------------------------]	◯	◯	◯
------------------------------------]	◯	◯	◯
------------------------------------]	◯	◯	◯
------------------------------------]	◯	◯	◯
------------------------------------]	◯	◯	◯
------------------------------------]	◯	◯	◯
------------------------------------]	◯	◯	◯
------------------------------------]	◯	◯	◯
------------------------------------]	◯	◯	◯
------------------------------------]	◯	◯	◯

NOTES:

Symptom Log

Description	MILD	MOD	SEVERE
------------------------------]	○	○	○
------------------------------]	○	○	○
------------------------------]	○	○	○
------------------------------]	○	○	○
------------------------------]	○	○	○
------------------------------]	○	○	○
------------------------------]	○	○	○
------------------------------]	○	○	○
------------------------------]	○	○	○
------------------------------]	○	○	○
------------------------------]	○	○	○

NOTES:

Symptom Log

Description	MILD	MOD	SEVERE
------------------------------------]	◯	◯	◯
------------------------------------]	◯	◯	◯
------------------------------------]	◯	◯	◯
------------------------------------]	◯	◯	◯
------------------------------------]	◯	◯	◯
------------------------------------]	◯	◯	◯
------------------------------------]	◯	◯	◯
------------------------------------]	◯	◯	◯
------------------------------------]	◯	◯	◯
------------------------------------]	◯	◯	◯
------------------------------------]	◯	◯	◯

NOTES:

Symptom Log

Description	MILD	MOD	SEVERE
-------------------------------]	◯	◯	◯
-------------------------------]	◯	◯	◯
-------------------------------]	◯	◯	◯
-------------------------------]	◯	◯	◯
-------------------------------]	◯	◯	◯
-------------------------------]	◯	◯	◯
-------------------------------]	◯	◯	◯
-------------------------------]	◯	◯	◯
-------------------------------]	◯	◯	◯
-------------------------------]	◯	◯	◯
-------------------------------]	◯	◯	◯

NOTES:

Symptom Log

Description	MILD	MOD	SEVERE
-------------------------------]	◯	◯	◯
-------------------------------]	◯	◯	◯
-------------------------------]	◯	◯	◯
-------------------------------]	◯	◯	◯
-------------------------------]	◯	◯	◯
-------------------------------]	◯	◯	◯
-------------------------------]	◯	◯	◯
-------------------------------]	◯	◯	◯
-------------------------------]	◯	◯	◯
-------------------------------]	◯	◯	◯
-------------------------------]	◯	◯	◯

NOTES:

Symptom Log

Description	MILD	MOD	SEVERE
----------------------------------]	◯	◯	◯
----------------------------------]	◯	◯	◯
----------------------------------]	◯	◯	◯
----------------------------------]	◯	◯	◯
----------------------------------]	◯	◯	◯
----------------------------------]	◯	◯	◯
----------------------------------]	◯	◯	◯
----------------------------------]	◯	◯	◯
----------------------------------]	◯	◯	◯
----------------------------------]	◯	◯	◯
----------------------------------]	◯	◯	◯

NOTES:

Symptom Log

Description	MILD	MOD	SEVERE
-------------------------------------]	◯	◯	◯
-------------------------------------]	◯	◯	◯
-------------------------------------]	◯	◯	◯
-------------------------------------]	◯	◯	◯
-------------------------------------]	◯	◯	◯
-------------------------------------]	◯	◯	◯
-------------------------------------]	◯	◯	◯
-------------------------------------]	◯	◯	◯
-------------------------------------]	◯	◯	◯
-------------------------------------]	◯	◯	◯
-------------------------------------]	◯	◯	◯

NOTES:

Symptom Log

Description	MILD	MOD	SEVERE
-----------------------------------]	◯	◯	◯
-----------------------------------]	◯	◯	◯
-----------------------------------]	◯	◯	◯
-----------------------------------]	◯	◯	◯
-----------------------------------]	◯	◯	◯
-----------------------------------]	◯	◯	◯
-----------------------------------]	◯	◯	◯
-----------------------------------]	◯	◯	◯
-----------------------------------]	◯	◯	◯
-----------------------------------]	◯	◯	◯
-----------------------------------]	◯	◯	◯

NOTES:

Symptom Log

Description	MILD	MOD	SEVERE
--------------------------------------]	◯	◯	◯
--------------------------------------]	◯	◯	◯
--------------------------------------]	◯	◯	◯
--------------------------------------]	◯	◯	◯
--------------------------------------]	◯	◯	◯
--------------------------------------]	◯	◯	◯
--------------------------------------]	◯	◯	◯
--------------------------------------]	◯	◯	◯
--------------------------------------]	◯	◯	◯
--------------------------------------]	◯	◯	◯
--------------------------------------]	◯	◯	◯

NOTES:

Symptom Log

Description	MILD	MOD	SEVERE
--------------------------------------]	◯	◯	◯
--------------------------------------]	◯	◯	◯
--------------------------------------]	◯	◯	◯
--------------------------------------]	◯	◯	◯
--------------------------------------]	◯	◯	◯
--------------------------------------]	◯	◯	◯
--------------------------------------]	◯	◯	◯
--------------------------------------]	◯	◯	◯
--------------------------------------]	◯	◯	◯
--------------------------------------]	◯	◯	◯
--------------------------------------]	◯	◯	◯

NOTES:

Symptom Log

Description	MILD	MOD	SEVERE
--------------------------------------]	○	○	○
--------------------------------------]	○	○	○
--------------------------------------]	○	○	○
--------------------------------------]	○	○	○
--------------------------------------]	○	○	○
--------------------------------------]	○	○	○
--------------------------------------]	○	○	○
--------------------------------------]	○	○	○
--------------------------------------]	○	○	○
--------------------------------------]	○	○	○
--------------------------------------]	○	○	○

NOTES:

Symptom Log

Description	MILD	MOD	SEVERE
--------------------------------------]	◯	◯	◯
--------------------------------------]	◯	◯	◯
--------------------------------------]	◯	◯	◯
--------------------------------------]	◯	◯	◯
--------------------------------------]	◯	◯	◯
--------------------------------------]	◯	◯	◯
--------------------------------------]	◯	◯	◯
--------------------------------------]	◯	◯	◯
--------------------------------------]	◯	◯	◯
--------------------------------------]	◯	◯	◯
--------------------------------------]	◯	◯	◯

NOTES:

Symptom Log

Description

	MILD	MOD	SEVERE

----------------------------------] ◯ ◯ ◯

----------------------------------] ◯ ◯ ◯

----------------------------------] ◯ ◯ ◯

----------------------------------] ◯ ◯ ◯

----------------------------------] ◯ ◯ ◯

----------------------------------] ◯ ◯ ◯

----------------------------------] ◯ ◯ ◯

----------------------------------] ◯ ◯ ◯

----------------------------------] ◯ ◯ ◯

----------------------------------] ◯ ◯ ◯

----------------------------------] ◯ ◯ ◯

NOTES:

Symptom Log

Description	MILD	MOD	SEVERE
-------------------------------------]	◯	◯	◯
-------------------------------------]	◯	◯	◯
-------------------------------------]	◯	◯	◯
-------------------------------------]	◯	◯	◯
-------------------------------------]	◯	◯	◯
-------------------------------------]	◯	◯	◯
-------------------------------------]	◯	◯	◯
-------------------------------------]	◯	◯	◯
-------------------------------------]	◯	◯	◯
-------------------------------------]	◯	◯	◯
-------------------------------------]	◯	◯	◯

NOTES:

Symptom Log

Description   MILD   MOD   SEVERE

-------------------------------------] ◯ ◯ ◯

-------------------------------------] ◯ ◯ ◯

-------------------------------------] ◯ ◯ ◯

-------------------------------------] ◯ ◯ ◯

-------------------------------------] ◯ ◯ ◯

-------------------------------------] ◯ ◯ ◯

-------------------------------------] ◯ ◯ ◯

-------------------------------------] ◯ ◯ ◯

-------------------------------------] ◯ ◯ ◯

-------------------------------------] ◯ ◯ ◯

-------------------------------------] ◯ ◯ ◯

NOTES:

Symptom Log

Description	MILD	MOD	SEVERE
-------------------------------]	◯	◯	◯
-------------------------------]	◯	◯	◯
-------------------------------]	◯	◯	◯
-------------------------------]	◯	◯	◯
-------------------------------]	◯	◯	◯
-------------------------------]	◯	◯	◯
-------------------------------]	◯	◯	◯
-------------------------------]	◯	◯	◯
-------------------------------]	◯	◯	◯
-------------------------------]	◯	◯	◯
-------------------------------]	◯	◯	◯

NOTES:

Symptom Log

Description   MILD   MOD   SEVERE

Description	MILD	MOD	SEVERE
------------------------------]	◯	◯	◯
------------------------------]	◯	◯	◯
------------------------------]	◯	◯	◯
------------------------------]	◯	◯	◯
------------------------------]	◯	◯	◯
------------------------------]	◯	◯	◯
------------------------------]	◯	◯	◯
------------------------------]	◯	◯	◯
------------------------------]	◯	◯	◯
------------------------------]	◯	◯	◯
------------------------------]	◯	◯	◯

NOTES:

Symptom Log

Description	MILD	MOD	SEVERE
-------------------------------------]	◯	◯	◯
-------------------------------------]	◯	◯	◯
-------------------------------------]	◯	◯	◯
-------------------------------------]	◯	◯	◯
-------------------------------------]	◯	◯	◯
-------------------------------------]	◯	◯	◯
-------------------------------------]	◯	◯	◯
-------------------------------------]	◯	◯	◯
-------------------------------------]	◯	◯	◯
-------------------------------------]	◯	◯	◯
-------------------------------------]	◯	◯	◯

NOTES:

Symptom Log

Description   MILD   MOD   SEVERE

-------------------------------------]   ◯   ◯   ◯

-------------------------------------]   ◯   ◯   ◯

-------------------------------------]   ◯   ◯   ◯

-------------------------------------]   ◯   ◯   ◯

-------------------------------------]   ◯   ◯   ◯

-------------------------------------]   ◯   ◯   ◯

-------------------------------------]   ◯   ◯   ◯

-------------------------------------]   ◯   ◯   ◯

-------------------------------------]   ◯   ◯   ◯

-------------------------------------]   ◯   ◯   ◯

-------------------------------------]   ◯   ◯   ◯

NOTES:

Symptom Log

Description	MILD	MOD	SEVERE
------------------------------------]	◯	◯	◯
------------------------------------]	◯	◯	◯
------------------------------------]	◯	◯	◯
------------------------------------]	◯	◯	◯
------------------------------------]	◯	◯	◯
------------------------------------]	◯	◯	◯
------------------------------------]	◯	◯	◯
------------------------------------]	◯	◯	◯
------------------------------------]	◯	◯	◯
------------------------------------]	◯	◯	◯
------------------------------------]	◯	◯	◯

NOTES:

Symptom Log

Description   MILD   MOD   SEVERE

-------------------------------------] ◯   ◯   ◯

-------------------------------------] ◯   ◯   ◯

-------------------------------------] ◯   ◯   ◯

-------------------------------------] ◯   ◯   ◯

-------------------------------------] ◯   ◯   ◯

-------------------------------------] ◯   ◯   ◯

-------------------------------------] ◯   ◯   ◯

-------------------------------------] ◯   ◯   ◯

-------------------------------------] ◯   ◯   ◯

-------------------------------------] ◯   ◯   ◯

-------------------------------------] ◯   ◯   ◯

NOTES:

Symptom Log

Description	MILD	MOD	SEVERE
------------------------------]	○	○	○
------------------------------]	○	○	○
------------------------------]	○	○	○
------------------------------]	○	○	○
------------------------------]	○	○	○
------------------------------]	○	○	○
------------------------------]	○	○	○
------------------------------]	○	○	○
------------------------------]	○	○	○
------------------------------]	○	○	○
------------------------------]	○	○	○

NOTES:

Symptom Log

Description	MILD	MOD	SEVERE
--------------------------------]	◯	◯	◯
--------------------------------]	◯	◯	◯
--------------------------------]	◯	◯	◯
--------------------------------]	◯	◯	◯
--------------------------------]	◯	◯	◯
--------------------------------]	◯	◯	◯
--------------------------------]	◯	◯	◯
--------------------------------]	◯	◯	◯
--------------------------------]	◯	◯	◯
--------------------------------]	◯	◯	◯
--------------------------------]	◯	◯	◯

NOTES:

Symptom Log

Description	MILD	MOD	SEVERE
----------------------------------]	◯	◯	◯
----------------------------------]	◯	◯	◯
----------------------------------]	◯	◯	◯
----------------------------------]	◯	◯	◯
----------------------------------]	◯	◯	◯
----------------------------------]	◯	◯	◯
----------------------------------]	◯	◯	◯
----------------------------------]	◯	◯	◯
----------------------------------]	◯	◯	◯
----------------------------------]	◯	◯	◯
----------------------------------]	◯	◯	◯

NOTES:

Symptom Log

Description   MILD   MOD   SEVERE

-------------------------------------]   ◯   ◯   ◯

-------------------------------------]   ◯   ◯   ◯

-------------------------------------]   ◯   ◯   ◯

-------------------------------------]   ◯   ◯   ◯

-------------------------------------]   ◯   ◯   ◯

-------------------------------------]   ◯   ◯   ◯

-------------------------------------]   ◯   ◯   ◯

-------------------------------------]   ◯   ◯   ◯

-------------------------------------]   ◯   ◯   ◯

-------------------------------------]   ◯   ◯   ◯

-------------------------------------]   ◯   ◯   ◯

NOTES:

Symptom Log

Description	MILD	MOD	SEVERE
------------------------------------]	○	○	○
------------------------------------]	○	○	○
------------------------------------]	○	○	○
------------------------------------]	○	○	○
------------------------------------]	○	○	○
------------------------------------]	○	○	○
------------------------------------]	○	○	○
------------------------------------]	○	○	○
------------------------------------]	○	○	○
------------------------------------]	○	○	○
------------------------------------]	○	○	○

NOTES:

Symptom Log

Description   MILD   MOD   SEVERE

------------------------------------]   ◯   ◯   ◯

------------------------------------]   ◯   ◯   ◯

------------------------------------]   ◯   ◯   ◯

------------------------------------]   ◯   ◯   ◯

------------------------------------]   ◯   ◯   ◯

------------------------------------]   ◯   ◯   ◯

------------------------------------]   ◯   ◯   ◯

------------------------------------]   ◯   ◯   ◯

------------------------------------]   ◯   ◯   ◯

------------------------------------]   ◯   ◯   ◯

------------------------------------]   ◯   ◯   ◯

NOTES:

Symptom Log

Description	MILD	MOD	SEVERE
----------------------------------]	◯	◯	◯
----------------------------------]	◯	◯	◯
----------------------------------]	◯	◯	◯
----------------------------------]	◯	◯	◯
----------------------------------]	◯	◯	◯
----------------------------------]	◯	◯	◯
----------------------------------]	◯	◯	◯
----------------------------------]	◯	◯	◯
----------------------------------]	◯	◯	◯
----------------------------------]	◯	◯	◯
----------------------------------]	◯	◯	◯

NOTES:

Symptom Log

Description	MILD	MOD	SEVERE
-------------------------------------]	◯	◯	◯
-------------------------------------]	◯	◯	◯
-------------------------------------]	◯	◯	◯
-------------------------------------]	◯	◯	◯
-------------------------------------]	◯	◯	◯
-------------------------------------]	◯	◯	◯
-------------------------------------]	◯	◯	◯
-------------------------------------]	◯	◯	◯
-------------------------------------]	◯	◯	◯
-------------------------------------]	◯	◯	◯
-------------------------------------]	◯	◯	◯

NOTES:

Symptom Log

Description   MILD   MOD   SEVERE

-------------------------------------]   ◯   ◯   ◯

-------------------------------------]   ◯   ◯   ◯

-------------------------------------]   ◯   ◯   ◯

-------------------------------------]   ◯   ◯   ◯

-------------------------------------]   ◯   ◯   ◯

-------------------------------------]   ◯   ◯   ◯

-------------------------------------]   ◯   ◯   ◯

-------------------------------------]   ◯   ◯   ◯

-------------------------------------]   ◯   ◯   ◯

-------------------------------------]   ◯   ◯   ◯

-------------------------------------]   ◯   ◯   ◯

NOTES:

Symptom Log

Description   MILD   MOD   SEVERE

----------------------------------] ◯ ◯ ◯

----------------------------------] ◯ ◯ ◯

----------------------------------] ◯ ◯ ◯

----------------------------------] ◯ ◯ ◯

----------------------------------] ◯ ◯ ◯

----------------------------------] ◯ ◯ ◯

----------------------------------] ◯ ◯ ◯

----------------------------------] ◯ ◯ ◯

----------------------------------] ◯ ◯ ◯

----------------------------------] ◯ ◯ ◯

----------------------------------] ◯ ◯ ◯

NOTES:

Symptom Log

Description	MILD	MOD	SEVERE
------------------------------]	◯	◯	◯
------------------------------]	◯	◯	◯
------------------------------]	◯	◯	◯
------------------------------]	◯	◯	◯
------------------------------]	◯	◯	◯
------------------------------]	◯	◯	◯
------------------------------]	◯	◯	◯
------------------------------]	◯	◯	◯
------------------------------]	◯	◯	◯
------------------------------]	◯	◯	◯
------------------------------]	◯	◯	◯

NOTES:

Symptom Log

Description

	MILD	MOD	SEVERE

-----------------------------------] ◯ ◯ ◯

-----------------------------------] ◯ ◯ ◯

-----------------------------------] ◯ ◯ ◯

-----------------------------------] ◯ ◯ ◯

-----------------------------------] ◯ ◯ ◯

-----------------------------------] ◯ ◯ ◯

-----------------------------------] ◯ ◯ ◯

-----------------------------------] ◯ ◯ ◯

-----------------------------------] ◯ ◯ ◯

-----------------------------------] ◯ ◯ ◯

-----------------------------------] ◯ ◯ ◯

NOTES:

Symptom Log

Description	MILD	MOD	SEVERE
----------------------------------]	○	○	○
----------------------------------]	○	○	○
----------------------------------]	○	○	○
----------------------------------]	○	○	○
----------------------------------]	○	○	○
----------------------------------]	○	○	○
----------------------------------]	○	○	○
----------------------------------]	○	○	○
----------------------------------]	○	○	○
----------------------------------]	○	○	○
----------------------------------]	○	○	○

NOTES:

Symptom Log

Description   MILD   MOD   SEVERE

--] ◯   ◯   ◯

--] ◯   ◯   ◯

--] ◯   ◯   ◯

--] ◯   ◯   ◯

--] ◯   ◯   ◯

--] ◯   ◯   ◯

--] ◯   ◯   ◯

--] ◯   ◯   ◯

--] ◯   ◯   ◯

--] ◯   ◯   ◯

--] ◯   ◯   ◯

NOTES:

It is important to take time and rest. Self Care is vital

Remember to just breathe...

Symptom Log

Description	MILD	MOD	SEVERE
---------------------------------------]	◯	◯	◯
---------------------------------------]	◯	◯	◯
---------------------------------------]	◯	◯	◯
---------------------------------------]	◯	◯	◯
---------------------------------------]	◯	◯	◯
---------------------------------------]	◯	◯	◯
---------------------------------------]	◯	◯	◯
---------------------------------------]	◯	◯	◯
---------------------------------------]	◯	◯	◯
---------------------------------------]	◯	◯	◯
---------------------------------------]	◯	◯	◯

NOTES:

Symptom Log

Description	MILD	MOD	SEVERE
------------------------------]	◯	◯	◯
------------------------------]	◯	◯	◯
------------------------------]	◯	◯	◯
------------------------------]	◯	◯	◯
------------------------------]	◯	◯	◯
------------------------------]	◯	◯	◯
------------------------------]	◯	◯	◯
------------------------------]	◯	◯	◯
------------------------------]	◯	◯	◯
------------------------------]	◯	◯	◯
------------------------------]	◯	◯	◯

NOTES:

Symptom Log

Description MILD   MOD   SEVERE

------------------------------------] ◯ ◯ ◯

------------------------------------] ◯ ◯ ◯

------------------------------------] ◯ ◯ ◯

------------------------------------] ◯ ◯ ◯

------------------------------------] ◯ ◯ ◯

------------------------------------] ◯ ◯ ◯

------------------------------------] ◯ ◯ ◯

------------------------------------] ◯ ◯ ◯

------------------------------------] ◯ ◯ ◯

------------------------------------] ◯ ◯ ◯

------------------------------------] ◯ ◯ ◯

NOTES:

Symptom Log

Description	MILD	MOD	SEVERE
------------------------------]	◯	◯	◯
------------------------------]	◯	◯	◯
------------------------------]	◯	◯	◯
------------------------------]	◯	◯	◯
------------------------------]	◯	◯	◯
------------------------------]	◯	◯	◯
------------------------------]	◯	◯	◯
------------------------------]	◯	◯	◯
------------------------------]	◯	◯	◯
------------------------------]	◯	◯	◯
------------------------------]	◯	◯	◯

NOTES:

Symptom Log

Description   MILD   MOD   SEVERE

-----------------------------------] ◯ ◯ ◯

-----------------------------------] ◯ ◯ ◯

-----------------------------------] ◯ ◯ ◯

-----------------------------------] ◯ ◯ ◯

-----------------------------------] ◯ ◯ ◯

-----------------------------------] ◯ ◯ ◯

-----------------------------------] ◯ ◯ ◯

-----------------------------------] ◯ ◯ ◯

-----------------------------------] ◯ ◯ ◯

-----------------------------------] ◯ ◯ ◯

-----------------------------------] ◯ ◯ ◯

NOTES:

Symptom Log

Description	MILD	MOD	SEVERE
------------------------------------]	◯	◯	◯
------------------------------------]	◯	◯	◯
------------------------------------]	◯	◯	◯
------------------------------------]	◯	◯	◯
------------------------------------]	◯	◯	◯
------------------------------------]	◯	◯	◯
------------------------------------]	◯	◯	◯
------------------------------------]	◯	◯	◯
------------------------------------]	◯	◯	◯
------------------------------------]	◯	◯	◯
------------------------------------]	◯	◯	◯

NOTES:

Symptom Log

Description   MILD   MOD   SEVERE

----------------------------------] ◯ ◯ ◯

----------------------------------] ◯ ◯ ◯

----------------------------------] ◯ ◯ ◯

----------------------------------] ◯ ◯ ◯

----------------------------------] ◯ ◯ ◯

----------------------------------] ◯ ◯ ◯

----------------------------------] ◯ ◯ ◯

----------------------------------] ◯ ◯ ◯

----------------------------------] ◯ ◯ ◯

----------------------------------] ◯ ◯ ◯

----------------------------------] ◯ ◯ ◯

NOTES:

Symptom Log

Description	MILD	MOD	SEVERE
----------------------]	◯	◯	◯
----------------------]	◯	◯	◯
----------------------]	◯	◯	◯
----------------------]	◯	◯	◯
----------------------]	◯	◯	◯
----------------------]	◯	◯	◯
----------------------]	◯	◯	◯
----------------------]	◯	◯	◯
----------------------]	◯	◯	◯
----------------------]	◯	◯	◯
----------------------]	◯	◯	◯

NOTES:

Symptom Log

Description	MILD	MOD	SEVERE
----------------------------------]	◯	◯	◯
----------------------------------]	◯	◯	◯
----------------------------------]	◯	◯	◯
----------------------------------]	◯	◯	◯
----------------------------------]	◯	◯	◯
----------------------------------]	◯	◯	◯
----------------------------------]	◯	◯	◯
----------------------------------]	◯	◯	◯
----------------------------------]	◯	◯	◯
----------------------------------]	◯	◯	◯
----------------------------------]	◯	◯	◯

NOTES:

Symptom Log

Description   MILD   MOD   SEVERE

----------------------------------]   ◯   ◯   ◯

----------------------------------]   ◯   ◯   ◯

----------------------------------]   ◯   ◯   ◯

----------------------------------]   ◯   ◯   ◯

----------------------------------]   ◯   ◯   ◯

----------------------------------]   ◯   ◯   ◯

----------------------------------]   ◯   ◯   ◯

----------------------------------]   ◯   ◯   ◯

----------------------------------]   ◯   ◯   ◯

----------------------------------]   ◯   ◯   ◯

----------------------------------]   ◯   ◯   ◯

NOTES:

Symptom Log

Description	MILD	MOD	SEVERE

-----------------------------------] ◯ ◯ ◯

-----------------------------------] ◯ ◯ ◯

-----------------------------------] ◯ ◯ ◯

-----------------------------------] ◯ ◯ ◯

-----------------------------------] ◯ ◯ ◯

-----------------------------------] ◯ ◯ ◯

-----------------------------------] ◯ ◯ ◯

-----------------------------------] ◯ ◯ ◯

-----------------------------------] ◯ ◯ ◯

-----------------------------------] ◯ ◯ ◯

-----------------------------------] ◯ ◯ ◯

NOTES:

Symptom Log

Description	MILD	MOD	SEVERE
------------------------------------]	◯	◯	◯
------------------------------------]	◯	◯	◯
------------------------------------]	◯	◯	◯
------------------------------------]	◯	◯	◯
------------------------------------]	◯	◯	◯
------------------------------------]	◯	◯	◯
------------------------------------]	◯	◯	◯
------------------------------------]	◯	◯	◯
------------------------------------]	◯	◯	◯
------------------------------------]	◯	◯	◯
------------------------------------]	◯	◯	◯

NOTES:

Symptom Log

Description	MILD	MOD	SEVERE
----------------------------]	◯	◯	◯
----------------------------]	◯	◯	◯
----------------------------]	◯	◯	◯
----------------------------]	◯	◯	◯
----------------------------]	◯	◯	◯
----------------------------]	◯	◯	◯
----------------------------]	◯	◯	◯
----------------------------]	◯	◯	◯
----------------------------]	◯	◯	◯
----------------------------]	◯	◯	◯
----------------------------]	◯	◯	◯

NOTES:

Symptom Log

Description	MILD	MOD	SEVERE
----------------------------------]	◯	◯	◯
----------------------------------]	◯	◯	◯
----------------------------------]	◯	◯	◯
----------------------------------]	◯	◯	◯
----------------------------------]	◯	◯	◯
----------------------------------]	◯	◯	◯
----------------------------------]	◯	◯	◯
----------------------------------]	◯	◯	◯
----------------------------------]	◯	◯	◯
----------------------------------]	◯	◯	◯
----------------------------------]	◯	◯	◯

NOTES:

Symptom Log

Description   MILD   MOD   SEVERE

-------------------------------------] ◯   ◯   ◯

-------------------------------------] ◯   ◯   ◯

-------------------------------------] ◯   ◯   ◯

-------------------------------------] ◯   ◯   ◯

-------------------------------------] ◯   ◯   ◯

-------------------------------------] ◯   ◯   ◯

-------------------------------------] ◯   ◯   ◯

-------------------------------------] ◯   ◯   ◯

-------------------------------------] ◯   ◯   ◯

-------------------------------------] ◯   ◯   ◯

-------------------------------------] ◯   ◯   ◯

NOTES:

Symptom Log

Description	MILD	MOD	SEVERE
------------------------------]	◯	◯	◯
------------------------------]	◯	◯	◯
------------------------------]	◯	◯	◯
------------------------------]	◯	◯	◯
------------------------------]	◯	◯	◯
------------------------------]	◯	◯	◯
------------------------------]	◯	◯	◯
------------------------------]	◯	◯	◯
------------------------------]	◯	◯	◯
------------------------------]	◯	◯	◯
------------------------------]	◯	◯	◯

NOTES:

Symptom Log

Description   MILD   MOD   SEVERE

-----------------------------------]   ◯   ◯   ◯

-----------------------------------]   ◯   ◯   ◯

-----------------------------------]   ◯   ◯   ◯

-----------------------------------]   ◯   ◯   ◯

-----------------------------------]   ◯   ◯   ◯

-----------------------------------]   ◯   ◯   ◯

-----------------------------------]   ◯   ◯   ◯

-----------------------------------]   ◯   ◯   ◯

-----------------------------------]   ◯   ◯   ◯

-----------------------------------]   ◯   ◯   ◯

-----------------------------------]   ◯   ◯   ◯

NOTES:

Symptom Log

Description	MILD	MOD	SEVERE
----------------------------------]	◯	◯	◯
----------------------------------]	◯	◯	◯
----------------------------------]	◯	◯	◯
----------------------------------]	◯	◯	◯
----------------------------------]	◯	◯	◯
----------------------------------]	◯	◯	◯
----------------------------------]	◯	◯	◯
----------------------------------]	◯	◯	◯
----------------------------------]	◯	◯	◯
----------------------------------]	◯	◯	◯
----------------------------------]	◯	◯	◯

NOTES:

Symptom Log

Description   MILD   MOD   SEVERE

------------------------------------] ◯ ◯ ◯

------------------------------------] ◯ ◯ ◯

------------------------------------] ◯ ◯ ◯

------------------------------------] ◯ ◯ ◯

------------------------------------] ◯ ◯ ◯

------------------------------------] ◯ ◯ ◯

------------------------------------] ◯ ◯ ◯

------------------------------------] ◯ ◯ ◯

------------------------------------] ◯ ◯ ◯

------------------------------------] ◯ ◯ ◯

------------------------------------] ◯ ◯ ◯

NOTES:

Symptom Log

Description	MILD	MOD	SEVERE
-------------------------------]	◯	◯	◯
-------------------------------]	◯	◯	◯
-------------------------------]	◯	◯	◯
-------------------------------]	◯	◯	◯
-------------------------------]	◯	◯	◯
-------------------------------]	◯	◯	◯
-------------------------------]	◯	◯	◯
-------------------------------]	◯	◯	◯
-------------------------------]	◯	◯	◯
-------------------------------]	◯	◯	◯
-------------------------------]	◯	◯	◯

NOTES:

Symptom Log

Description	MILD	MOD	SEVERE
------------------------------------]	◯	◯	◯
------------------------------------]	◯	◯	◯
------------------------------------]	◯	◯	◯
------------------------------------]	◯	◯	◯
------------------------------------]	◯	◯	◯
------------------------------------]	◯	◯	◯
------------------------------------]	◯	◯	◯
------------------------------------]	◯	◯	◯
------------------------------------]	◯	◯	◯
------------------------------------]	◯	◯	◯
------------------------------------]	◯	◯	◯

NOTES:

Symptom Log

Description	MILD	MOD	SEVERE
------------------------------------]	◯	◯	◯
------------------------------------]	◯	◯	◯
------------------------------------]	◯	◯	◯
------------------------------------]	◯	◯	◯
------------------------------------]	◯	◯	◯
------------------------------------]	◯	◯	◯
------------------------------------]	◯	◯	◯
------------------------------------]	◯	◯	◯
------------------------------------]	◯	◯	◯
------------------------------------]	◯	◯	◯
------------------------------------]	◯	◯	◯

NOTES:

Symptom Log

Description	MILD	MOD	SEVERE
------------------------------------]	◯	◯	◯
------------------------------------]	◯	◯	◯
------------------------------------]	◯	◯	◯
------------------------------------]	◯	◯	◯
------------------------------------]	◯	◯	◯
------------------------------------]	◯	◯	◯
------------------------------------]	◯	◯	◯
------------------------------------]	◯	◯	◯
------------------------------------]	◯	◯	◯
------------------------------------]	◯	◯	◯
------------------------------------]	◯	◯	◯

NOTES:

Symptom Log

Description	MILD	MOD	SEVERE
--------------------------------]	◯	◯	◯
--------------------------------]	◯	◯	◯
--------------------------------]	◯	◯	◯
--------------------------------]	◯	◯	◯
--------------------------------]	◯	◯	◯
--------------------------------]	◯	◯	◯
--------------------------------]	◯	◯	◯
--------------------------------]	◯	◯	◯
--------------------------------]	◯	◯	◯
--------------------------------]	◯	◯	◯
--------------------------------]	◯	◯	◯

NOTES:

Symptom Log

Description	MILD	MOD	SEVERE
------------------------------------]	◯	◯	◯
------------------------------------]	◯	◯	◯
------------------------------------]	◯	◯	◯
------------------------------------]	◯	◯	◯
------------------------------------]	◯	◯	◯
------------------------------------]	◯	◯	◯
------------------------------------]	◯	◯	◯
------------------------------------]	◯	◯	◯
------------------------------------]	◯	◯	◯
------------------------------------]	◯	◯	◯
------------------------------------]	◯	◯	◯

NOTES:

Symptom Log

Description	MILD	MOD	SEVERE
-------------------------------]	◯	◯	◯
-------------------------------]	◯	◯	◯
-------------------------------]	◯	◯	◯
-------------------------------]	◯	◯	◯
-------------------------------]	◯	◯	◯
-------------------------------]	◯	◯	◯
-------------------------------]	◯	◯	◯
-------------------------------]	◯	◯	◯
-------------------------------]	◯	◯	◯
-------------------------------]	◯	◯	◯
-------------------------------]	◯	◯	◯

NOTES:

Symptom Log

Description   MILD   MOD   SEVERE

------------------------------------]   ◯   ◯   ◯

------------------------------------]   ◯   ◯   ◯

------------------------------------]   ◯   ◯   ◯

------------------------------------]   ◯   ◯   ◯

------------------------------------]   ◯   ◯   ◯

------------------------------------]   ◯   ◯   ◯

------------------------------------]   ◯   ◯   ◯

------------------------------------]   ◯   ◯   ◯

------------------------------------]   ◯   ◯   ◯

------------------------------------]   ◯   ◯   ◯

------------------------------------]   ◯   ◯   ◯

NOTES:

Symptom Log

Description   MILD   MOD   SEVERE

-------------------------------] ◯ ◯ ◯

-------------------------------] ◯ ◯ ◯

-------------------------------] ◯ ◯ ◯

-------------------------------] ◯ ◯ ◯

-------------------------------] ◯ ◯ ◯

-------------------------------] ◯ ◯ ◯

-------------------------------] ◯ ◯ ◯

-------------------------------] ◯ ◯ ◯

-------------------------------] ◯ ◯ ◯

-------------------------------] ◯ ◯ ◯

-------------------------------] ◯ ◯ ◯

NOTES:

Symptom Log

Description	MILD	MOD	SEVERE
----------------------------------]	◯	◯	◯
----------------------------------]	◯	◯	◯
----------------------------------]	◯	◯	◯
----------------------------------]	◯	◯	◯
----------------------------------]	◯	◯	◯
----------------------------------]	◯	◯	◯
----------------------------------]	◯	◯	◯
----------------------------------]	◯	◯	◯
----------------------------------]	◯	◯	◯
----------------------------------]	◯	◯	◯
----------------------------------]	◯	◯	◯

NOTES:

Symptom Log

Description	MILD	MOD	SEVERE
----------------------------------]	◯	◯	◯
----------------------------------]	◯	◯	◯
----------------------------------]	◯	◯	◯
----------------------------------]	◯	◯	◯
----------------------------------]	◯	◯	◯
----------------------------------]	◯	◯	◯
----------------------------------]	◯	◯	◯
----------------------------------]	◯	◯	◯
----------------------------------]	◯	◯	◯
----------------------------------]	◯	◯	◯
----------------------------------]	◯	◯	◯

NOTES:

Symptom Log

Description	MILD	MOD	SEVERE
------------------------------------]	◯	◯	◯
------------------------------------]	◯	◯	◯
------------------------------------]	◯	◯	◯
------------------------------------]	◯	◯	◯
------------------------------------]	◯	◯	◯
------------------------------------]	◯	◯	◯
------------------------------------]	◯	◯	◯
------------------------------------]	◯	◯	◯
------------------------------------]	◯	◯	◯
------------------------------------]	◯	◯	◯
------------------------------------]	◯	◯	◯

NOTES:

Symptom Log

Description	MILD	MOD	SEVERE
----------------------------------]	◯	◯	◯
----------------------------------]	◯	◯	◯
----------------------------------]	◯	◯	◯
----------------------------------]	◯	◯	◯
----------------------------------]	◯	◯	◯
----------------------------------]	◯	◯	◯
----------------------------------]	◯	◯	◯
----------------------------------]	◯	◯	◯
----------------------------------]	◯	◯	◯
----------------------------------]	◯	◯	◯
----------------------------------]	◯	◯	◯

NOTES:

Symptom Log

Description	MILD	MOD	SEVERE
-------------------------------------]	◯	◯	◯
-------------------------------------]	◯	◯	◯
-------------------------------------]	◯	◯	◯
-------------------------------------]	◯	◯	◯
-------------------------------------]	◯	◯	◯
-------------------------------------]	◯	◯	◯
-------------------------------------]	◯	◯	◯
-------------------------------------]	◯	◯	◯
-------------------------------------]	◯	◯	◯
-------------------------------------]	◯	◯	◯
-------------------------------------]	◯	◯	◯

NOTES:

Symptom Log

Description	MILD	MOD	SEVERE
----------------------------]	◯	◯	◯
----------------------------]	◯	◯	◯
----------------------------]	◯	◯	◯
----------------------------]	◯	◯	◯
----------------------------]	◯	◯	◯
----------------------------]	◯	◯	◯
----------------------------]	◯	◯	◯
----------------------------]	◯	◯	◯
----------------------------]	◯	◯	◯
----------------------------]	◯	◯	◯
----------------------------]	◯	◯	◯

NOTES:

Symptom Log

Description	MILD	MOD	SEVERE
--]	◯	◯	◯
--]	◯	◯	◯
--]	◯	◯	◯
--]	◯	◯	◯
--]	◯	◯	◯
--]	◯	◯	◯
--]	◯	◯	◯
--]	◯	◯	◯
--]	◯	◯	◯
--]	◯	◯	◯
--]	◯	◯	◯

NOTES:

Symptom Log

Description	MILD	MOD	SEVERE
-------------------------------]	○	○	○
-------------------------------]	○	○	○
-------------------------------]	○	○	○
-------------------------------]	○	○	○
-------------------------------]	○	○	○
-------------------------------]	○	○	○
-------------------------------]	○	○	○
-------------------------------]	○	○	○
-------------------------------]	○	○	○
-------------------------------]	○	○	○
-------------------------------]	○	○	○

NOTES:

Symptom Log

Description   MILD   MOD   SEVERE

-------------------------------------]   ◯   ◯   ◯

-------------------------------------]   ◯   ◯   ◯

-------------------------------------]   ◯   ◯   ◯

-------------------------------------]   ◯   ◯   ◯

-------------------------------------]   ◯   ◯   ◯

-------------------------------------]   ◯   ◯   ◯

-------------------------------------]   ◯   ◯   ◯

-------------------------------------]   ◯   ◯   ◯

-------------------------------------]   ◯   ◯   ◯

-------------------------------------]   ◯   ◯   ◯

-------------------------------------]   ◯   ◯   ◯

NOTES:

Symptom Log

Description	MILD	MOD	SEVERE
----------------------------------]	◯	◯	◯
----------------------------------]	◯	◯	◯
----------------------------------]	◯	◯	◯
----------------------------------]	◯	◯	◯
----------------------------------]	◯	◯	◯
----------------------------------]	◯	◯	◯
----------------------------------]	◯	◯	◯
----------------------------------]	◯	◯	◯
----------------------------------]	◯	◯	◯
----------------------------------]	◯	◯	◯
----------------------------------]	◯	◯	◯

NOTES:

Symptom Log

Description	MILD	MOD	SEVERE
------------------------------]	◯	◯	◯
------------------------------]	◯	◯	◯
------------------------------]	◯	◯	◯
------------------------------]	◯	◯	◯
------------------------------]	◯	◯	◯
------------------------------]	◯	◯	◯
------------------------------]	◯	◯	◯
------------------------------]	◯	◯	◯
------------------------------]	◯	◯	◯
------------------------------]	◯	◯	◯
------------------------------]	◯	◯	◯

NOTES:

Symptom Log

Description	MILD	MOD	SEVERE
----------------------------------]	◯	◯	◯
----------------------------------]	◯	◯	◯
----------------------------------]	◯	◯	◯
----------------------------------]	◯	◯	◯
----------------------------------]	◯	◯	◯
----------------------------------]	◯	◯	◯
----------------------------------]	◯	◯	◯
----------------------------------]	◯	◯	◯
----------------------------------]	◯	◯	◯
----------------------------------]	◯	◯	◯
----------------------------------]	◯	◯	◯

NOTES:

Symptom Log

Description

	MILD	MOD	SEVERE
--------------------------------]	◯	◯	◯
--------------------------------]	◯	◯	◯
--------------------------------]	◯	◯	◯
--------------------------------]	◯	◯	◯
--------------------------------]	◯	◯	◯
--------------------------------]	◯	◯	◯
--------------------------------]	◯	◯	◯
--------------------------------]	◯	◯	◯
--------------------------------]	◯	◯	◯
--------------------------------]	◯	◯	◯
--------------------------------]	◯	◯	◯

NOTES:

Symptom Log

Description	MILD	MOD	SEVERE
------------------------------]	◯	◯	◯
------------------------------]	◯	◯	◯
------------------------------]	◯	◯	◯
------------------------------]	◯	◯	◯
------------------------------]	◯	◯	◯
------------------------------]	◯	◯	◯
------------------------------]	◯	◯	◯
------------------------------]	◯	◯	◯
------------------------------]	◯	◯	◯
------------------------------]	◯	◯	◯
------------------------------]	◯	◯	◯

NOTES:

Symptom Log

Description	MILD	MOD	SEVERE
---------------------------------]	◯	◯	◯
---------------------------------]	◯	◯	◯
---------------------------------]	◯	◯	◯
---------------------------------]	◯	◯	◯
---------------------------------]	◯	◯	◯
---------------------------------]	◯	◯	◯
---------------------------------]	◯	◯	◯
---------------------------------]	◯	◯	◯
---------------------------------]	◯	◯	◯
---------------------------------]	◯	◯	◯
---------------------------------]	◯	◯	◯

NOTES:

Symptom Log

Description	MILD	MOD	SEVERE
-------------------------------]	◯	◯	◯
-------------------------------]	◯	◯	◯
-------------------------------]	◯	◯	◯
-------------------------------]	◯	◯	◯
-------------------------------]	◯	◯	◯
-------------------------------]	◯	◯	◯
-------------------------------]	◯	◯	◯
-------------------------------]	◯	◯	◯
-------------------------------]	◯	◯	◯
-------------------------------]	◯	◯	◯
-------------------------------]	◯	◯	◯

NOTES:

Symptom Log

Description	MILD	MOD	SEVERE
------------------------------]	◯	◯	◯
------------------------------]	◯	◯	◯
------------------------------]	◯	◯	◯
------------------------------]	◯	◯	◯
------------------------------]	◯	◯	◯
------------------------------]	◯	◯	◯
------------------------------]	◯	◯	◯
------------------------------]	◯	◯	◯
------------------------------]	◯	◯	◯
------------------------------]	◯	◯	◯
------------------------------]	◯	◯	◯

NOTES:

Symptom Log

Description	MILD	MOD	SEVERE
------------------------------]	○	○	○
------------------------------]	○	○	○
------------------------------]	○	○	○
------------------------------]	○	○	○
------------------------------]	○	○	○
------------------------------]	○	○	○
------------------------------]	○	○	○
------------------------------]	○	○	○
------------------------------]	○	○	○
------------------------------]	○	○	○
------------------------------]	○	○	○

NOTES:

Symptom Log

Description   MILD   MOD   SEVERE

----------------------------------]   ◯   ◯   ◯

----------------------------------]   ◯   ◯   ◯

----------------------------------]   ◯   ◯   ◯

----------------------------------]   ◯   ◯   ◯

----------------------------------]   ◯   ◯   ◯

----------------------------------]   ◯   ◯   ◯

----------------------------------]   ◯   ◯   ◯

----------------------------------]   ◯   ◯   ◯

----------------------------------]   ◯   ◯   ◯

----------------------------------]   ◯   ◯   ◯

----------------------------------]   ◯   ◯   ◯

NOTES:

Symptom Log

Description	MILD	MOD	SEVERE
-------------------------------]	○	○	○
-------------------------------]	○	○	○
-------------------------------]	○	○	○
-------------------------------]	○	○	○
-------------------------------]	○	○	○
-------------------------------]	○	○	○
-------------------------------]	○	○	○
-------------------------------]	○	○	○
-------------------------------]	○	○	○
-------------------------------]	○	○	○
-------------------------------]	○	○	○

NOTES:

Symptom Log

Description   MILD   MOD   SEVERE

--------------------------------]   ◯   ◯   ◯

--------------------------------]   ◯   ◯   ◯

--------------------------------]   ◯   ◯   ◯

--------------------------------]   ◯   ◯   ◯

--------------------------------]   ◯   ◯   ◯

--------------------------------]   ◯   ◯   ◯

--------------------------------]   ◯   ◯   ◯

--------------------------------]   ◯   ◯   ◯

--------------------------------]   ◯   ◯   ◯

--------------------------------]   ◯   ◯   ◯

--------------------------------]   ◯   ◯   ◯

NOTES:

Symptom Log

Description	MILD	MOD	SEVERE
---------------------------------]	◯	◯	◯
---------------------------------]	◯	◯	◯
---------------------------------]	◯	◯	◯
---------------------------------]	◯	◯	◯
---------------------------------]	◯	◯	◯
---------------------------------]	◯	◯	◯
---------------------------------]	◯	◯	◯
---------------------------------]	◯	◯	◯
---------------------------------]	◯	◯	◯
---------------------------------]	◯	◯	◯
---------------------------------]	◯	◯	◯

NOTES:

Symptom Log

Description	MILD	MOD	SEVERE
--------------------------------]	◯	◯	◯
--------------------------------]	◯	◯	◯
--------------------------------]	◯	◯	◯
--------------------------------]	◯	◯	◯
--------------------------------]	◯	◯	◯
--------------------------------]	◯	◯	◯
--------------------------------]	◯	◯	◯
--------------------------------]	◯	◯	◯
--------------------------------]	◯	◯	◯
--------------------------------]	◯	◯	◯
--------------------------------]	◯	◯	◯

NOTES:

Symptom Log

Description	MILD	MOD	SEVERE
----------------------------------]	○	○	○
----------------------------------]	○	○	○
----------------------------------]	○	○	○
----------------------------------]	○	○	○
----------------------------------]	○	○	○
----------------------------------]	○	○	○
----------------------------------]	○	○	○
----------------------------------]	○	○	○
----------------------------------]	○	○	○
----------------------------------]	○	○	○
----------------------------------]	○	○	○

NOTES:

Symptom Log

Description	MILD	MOD	SEVERE
----------------------------------]	◯	◯	◯
----------------------------------]	◯	◯	◯
----------------------------------]	◯	◯	◯
----------------------------------]	◯	◯	◯
----------------------------------]	◯	◯	◯
----------------------------------]	◯	◯	◯
----------------------------------]	◯	◯	◯
----------------------------------]	◯	◯	◯
----------------------------------]	◯	◯	◯
----------------------------------]	◯	◯	◯
----------------------------------]	◯	◯	◯

NOTES:

Symptom Log

Description   MILD   MOD   SEVERE

-----------------------------------]   ◯   ◯   ◯

-----------------------------------]   ◯   ◯   ◯

-----------------------------------]   ◯   ◯   ◯

-----------------------------------]   ◯   ◯   ◯

-----------------------------------]   ◯   ◯   ◯

-----------------------------------]   ◯   ◯   ◯

-----------------------------------]   ◯   ◯   ◯

-----------------------------------]   ◯   ◯   ◯

-----------------------------------]   ◯   ◯   ◯

-----------------------------------]   ◯   ◯   ◯

-----------------------------------]   ◯   ◯   ◯

NOTES:

Symptom Log

Description   MILD   MOD   SEVERE

------------------------------------]   ◯   ◯   ◯

------------------------------------]   ◯   ◯   ◯

------------------------------------]   ◯   ◯   ◯

------------------------------------]   ◯   ◯   ◯

------------------------------------]   ◯   ◯   ◯

------------------------------------]   ◯   ◯   ◯

------------------------------------]   ◯   ◯   ◯

------------------------------------]   ◯   ◯   ◯

------------------------------------]   ◯   ◯   ◯

------------------------------------]   ◯   ◯   ◯

------------------------------------]   ◯   ◯   ◯

NOTES:

Symptom Log

Description	MILD	MOD	SEVERE
----------------------------------]	◯	◯	◯
----------------------------------]	◯	◯	◯
----------------------------------]	◯	◯	◯
----------------------------------]	◯	◯	◯
----------------------------------]	◯	◯	◯
----------------------------------]	◯	◯	◯
----------------------------------]	◯	◯	◯
----------------------------------]	◯	◯	◯
----------------------------------]	◯	◯	◯
----------------------------------]	◯	◯	◯
----------------------------------]	◯	◯	◯

NOTES:

Symptom Log

Description	MILD	MOD	SEVERE
------------------------------]	◯	◯	◯
------------------------------]	◯	◯	◯
------------------------------]	◯	◯	◯
------------------------------]	◯	◯	◯
------------------------------]	◯	◯	◯
------------------------------]	◯	◯	◯
------------------------------]	◯	◯	◯
------------------------------]	◯	◯	◯
------------------------------]	◯	◯	◯
------------------------------]	◯	◯	◯
------------------------------]	◯	◯	◯

NOTES:

Symptom Log

Description	MILD	MOD	SEVERE
----------------------------------]	◯	◯	◯
----------------------------------]	◯	◯	◯
----------------------------------]	◯	◯	◯
----------------------------------]	◯	◯	◯
----------------------------------]	◯	◯	◯
----------------------------------]	◯	◯	◯
----------------------------------]	◯	◯	◯
----------------------------------]	◯	◯	◯
----------------------------------]	◯	◯	◯
----------------------------------]	◯	◯	◯
----------------------------------]	◯	◯	◯

NOTES:

Symptom Log

Description	MILD	MOD	SEVERE
------------------------------------]	◯	◯	◯
------------------------------------]	◯	◯	◯
------------------------------------]	◯	◯	◯
------------------------------------]	◯	◯	◯
------------------------------------]	◯	◯	◯
------------------------------------]	◯	◯	◯
------------------------------------]	◯	◯	◯
------------------------------------]	◯	◯	◯
------------------------------------]	◯	◯	◯
------------------------------------]	◯	◯	◯
------------------------------------]	◯	◯	◯

NOTES:

Symptom Log

Description   MILD   MOD   SEVERE

---------------------------------] ◯ ◯ ◯

---------------------------------] ◯ ◯ ◯

---------------------------------] ◯ ◯ ◯

---------------------------------] ◯ ◯ ◯

---------------------------------] ◯ ◯ ◯

---------------------------------] ◯ ◯ ◯

---------------------------------] ◯ ◯ ◯

---------------------------------] ◯ ◯ ◯

---------------------------------] ◯ ◯ ◯

---------------------------------] ◯ ◯ ◯

---------------------------------] ◯ ◯ ◯

NOTES:

Symptom Log

Description	MILD	MOD	SEVERE
--------------------------------]	◯	◯	◯
--------------------------------]	◯	◯	◯
--------------------------------]	◯	◯	◯
--------------------------------]	◯	◯	◯
--------------------------------]	◯	◯	◯
--------------------------------]	◯	◯	◯
--------------------------------]	◯	◯	◯
--------------------------------]	◯	◯	◯
--------------------------------]	◯	◯	◯
--------------------------------]	◯	◯	◯
--------------------------------]	◯	◯	◯

NOTES:

Symptom Log

Description	MILD	MOD	SEVERE
------------------------------]	◯	◯	◯
------------------------------]	◯	◯	◯
------------------------------]	◯	◯	◯
------------------------------]	◯	◯	◯
------------------------------]	◯	◯	◯
------------------------------]	◯	◯	◯
------------------------------]	◯	◯	◯
------------------------------]	◯	◯	◯
------------------------------]	◯	◯	◯
------------------------------]	◯	◯	◯
------------------------------]	◯	◯	◯

NOTES:

Symptom Log

Description	MILD	MOD	SEVERE
----------------------------------]	◯	◯	◯
----------------------------------]	◯	◯	◯
----------------------------------]	◯	◯	◯
----------------------------------]	◯	◯	◯
----------------------------------]	◯	◯	◯
----------------------------------]	◯	◯	◯
----------------------------------]	◯	◯	◯
----------------------------------]	◯	◯	◯
----------------------------------]	◯	◯	◯
----------------------------------]	◯	◯	◯
----------------------------------]	◯	◯	◯

NOTES:

Symptom Log

Description	MILD	MOD	SEVERE
---------------------------------]	◯	◯	◯
---------------------------------]	◯	◯	◯
---------------------------------]	◯	◯	◯
---------------------------------]	◯	◯	◯
---------------------------------]	◯	◯	◯
---------------------------------]	◯	◯	◯
---------------------------------]	◯	◯	◯
---------------------------------]	◯	◯	◯
---------------------------------]	◯	◯	◯
---------------------------------]	◯	◯	◯
---------------------------------]	◯	◯	◯

NOTES:

Symptom Log

Description   MILD   MOD   SEVERE

-------------------------------------] ◯ ◯ ◯

-------------------------------------] ◯ ◯ ◯

-------------------------------------] ◯ ◯ ◯

-------------------------------------] ◯ ◯ ◯

-------------------------------------] ◯ ◯ ◯

-------------------------------------] ◯ ◯ ◯

-------------------------------------] ◯ ◯ ◯

-------------------------------------] ◯ ◯ ◯

-------------------------------------] ◯ ◯ ◯

-------------------------------------] ◯ ◯ ◯

-------------------------------------] ◯ ◯ ◯

NOTES:

Symptom Log

Description	MILD	MOD	SEVERE
------------------------------------]	◯	◯	◯
------------------------------------]	◯	◯	◯
------------------------------------]	◯	◯	◯
------------------------------------]	◯	◯	◯
------------------------------------]	◯	◯	◯
------------------------------------]	◯	◯	◯
------------------------------------]	◯	◯	◯
------------------------------------]	◯	◯	◯
------------------------------------]	◯	◯	◯
------------------------------------]	◯	◯	◯
------------------------------------]	◯	◯	◯

NOTES:

Symptom Log

Description	MILD	MOD	SEVERE
-----------------------------------]	◯	◯	◯
-----------------------------------]	◯	◯	◯
-----------------------------------]	◯	◯	◯
-----------------------------------]	◯	◯	◯
-----------------------------------]	◯	◯	◯
-----------------------------------]	◯	◯	◯
-----------------------------------]	◯	◯	◯
-----------------------------------]	◯	◯	◯
-----------------------------------]	◯	◯	◯
-----------------------------------]	◯	◯	◯
-----------------------------------]	◯	◯	◯

NOTES:

Symptom Log

Description	MILD	MOD	SEVERE
--------------------------------------]	◯	◯	◯
--------------------------------------]	◯	◯	◯
--------------------------------------]	◯	◯	◯
--------------------------------------]	◯	◯	◯
--------------------------------------]	◯	◯	◯
--------------------------------------]	◯	◯	◯
--------------------------------------]	◯	◯	◯
--------------------------------------]	◯	◯	◯
--------------------------------------]	◯	◯	◯
--------------------------------------]	◯	◯	◯
--------------------------------------]	◯	◯	◯

NOTES:

Symptom Log

Description	MILD	MOD	SEVERE
----------------------------------]	⭕	⭕	⭕
----------------------------------]	⭕	⭕	⭕
----------------------------------]	⭕	⭕	⭕
----------------------------------]	⭕	⭕	⭕
----------------------------------]	⭕	⭕	⭕
----------------------------------]	⭕	⭕	⭕
----------------------------------]	⭕	⭕	⭕
----------------------------------]	⭕	⭕	⭕
----------------------------------]	⭕	⭕	⭕
----------------------------------]	⭕	⭕	⭕
----------------------------------]	⭕	⭕	⭕

NOTES:

Symptom Log

Description	MILD	MOD	SEVERE
--------------------------------]	◯	◯	◯
--------------------------------]	◯	◯	◯
--------------------------------]	◯	◯	◯
--------------------------------]	◯	◯	◯
--------------------------------]	◯	◯	◯
--------------------------------]	◯	◯	◯
--------------------------------]	◯	◯	◯
--------------------------------]	◯	◯	◯
--------------------------------]	◯	◯	◯
--------------------------------]	◯	◯	◯
--------------------------------]	◯	◯	◯

NOTES:

Symptom Log

Description   MILD   MOD   SEVERE

-----------------------------------] ◯ ◯ ◯

-----------------------------------] ◯ ◯ ◯

-----------------------------------] ◯ ◯ ◯

-----------------------------------] ◯ ◯ ◯

-----------------------------------] ◯ ◯ ◯

-----------------------------------] ◯ ◯ ◯

-----------------------------------] ◯ ◯ ◯

-----------------------------------] ◯ ◯ ◯

-----------------------------------] ◯ ◯ ◯

-----------------------------------] ◯ ◯ ◯

-----------------------------------] ◯ ◯ ◯

NOTES:

Symptom Log

Description	MILD	MOD	SEVERE
---------------------------------]	◯	◯	◯
---------------------------------]	◯	◯	◯
---------------------------------]	◯	◯	◯
---------------------------------]	◯	◯	◯
---------------------------------]	◯	◯	◯
---------------------------------]	◯	◯	◯
---------------------------------]	◯	◯	◯
---------------------------------]	◯	◯	◯
---------------------------------]	◯	◯	◯
---------------------------------]	◯	◯	◯
---------------------------------]	◯	◯	◯

NOTES:

Symptom Log

Description   MILD   MOD   SEVERE

Description	MILD	MOD	SEVERE
-------------------------------------]	◯	◯	◯
-------------------------------------]	◯	◯	◯
-------------------------------------]	◯	◯	◯
-------------------------------------]	◯	◯	◯
-------------------------------------]	◯	◯	◯
-------------------------------------]	◯	◯	◯
-------------------------------------]	◯	◯	◯
-------------------------------------]	◯	◯	◯
-------------------------------------]	◯	◯	◯
-------------------------------------]	◯	◯	◯
-------------------------------------]	◯	◯	◯

NOTES:

Symptom Log

Description	MILD	MOD	SEVERE
-----------------------------------]	◯	◯	◯
-----------------------------------]	◯	◯	◯
-----------------------------------]	◯	◯	◯
-----------------------------------]	◯	◯	◯
-----------------------------------]	◯	◯	◯
-----------------------------------]	◯	◯	◯
-----------------------------------]	◯	◯	◯
-----------------------------------]	◯	◯	◯
-----------------------------------]	◯	◯	◯
-----------------------------------]	◯	◯	◯
-----------------------------------]	◯	◯	◯

NOTES:

Symptom Log

Description	MILD	MOD	SEVERE
--------------------------------]	◯	◯	◯
--------------------------------]	◯	◯	◯
--------------------------------]	◯	◯	◯
--------------------------------]	◯	◯	◯
--------------------------------]	◯	◯	◯
--------------------------------]	◯	◯	◯
--------------------------------]	◯	◯	◯
--------------------------------]	◯	◯	◯
--------------------------------]	◯	◯	◯
--------------------------------]	◯	◯	◯
--------------------------------]	◯	◯	◯

NOTES:

Symptom Log

Description	MILD	MOD	SEVERE
--------------------------------]	◯	◯	◯
--------------------------------]	◯	◯	◯
--------------------------------]	◯	◯	◯
--------------------------------]	◯	◯	◯
--------------------------------]	◯	◯	◯
--------------------------------]	◯	◯	◯
--------------------------------]	◯	◯	◯
--------------------------------]	◯	◯	◯
--------------------------------]	◯	◯	◯
--------------------------------]	◯	◯	◯
--------------------------------]	◯	◯	◯

NOTES:

Symptom Log

Description	MILD	MOD	SEVERE
------------------------------------]	◯	◯	◯
------------------------------------]	◯	◯	◯
------------------------------------]	◯	◯	◯
------------------------------------]	◯	◯	◯
------------------------------------]	◯	◯	◯
------------------------------------]	◯	◯	◯
------------------------------------]	◯	◯	◯
------------------------------------]	◯	◯	◯
------------------------------------]	◯	◯	◯
------------------------------------]	◯	◯	◯
------------------------------------]	◯	◯	◯

NOTES:

Symptom Log

Description	MILD	MOD	SEVERE
----------------------------------]	○	○	○
----------------------------------]	○	○	○
----------------------------------]	○	○	○
----------------------------------]	○	○	○
----------------------------------]	○	○	○
----------------------------------]	○	○	○
----------------------------------]	○	○	○
----------------------------------]	○	○	○
----------------------------------]	○	○	○
----------------------------------]	○	○	○
----------------------------------]	○	○	○

NOTES:

Symptom Log

Description	MILD	MOD	SEVERE
--------------------------------]	◯	◯	◯
--------------------------------]	◯	◯	◯
--------------------------------]	◯	◯	◯
--------------------------------]	◯	◯	◯
--------------------------------]	◯	◯	◯
--------------------------------]	◯	◯	◯
--------------------------------]	◯	◯	◯
--------------------------------]	◯	◯	◯
--------------------------------]	◯	◯	◯
--------------------------------]	◯	◯	◯
--------------------------------]	◯	◯	◯

NOTES:

Symptom Log

Description	MILD	MOD	SEVERE
------------------------------]	◯	◯	◯
------------------------------]	◯	◯	◯
------------------------------]	◯	◯	◯
------------------------------]	◯	◯	◯
------------------------------]	◯	◯	◯
------------------------------]	◯	◯	◯
------------------------------]	◯	◯	◯
------------------------------]	◯	◯	◯
------------------------------]	◯	◯	◯
------------------------------]	◯	◯	◯
------------------------------]	◯	◯	◯

NOTES:

Symptom Log

Description   MILD   MOD   SEVERE

----------------------------------] ◯ ◯ ◯

----------------------------------] ◯ ◯ ◯

----------------------------------] ◯ ◯ ◯

----------------------------------] ◯ ◯ ◯

----------------------------------] ◯ ◯ ◯

----------------------------------] ◯ ◯ ◯

----------------------------------] ◯ ◯ ◯

----------------------------------] ◯ ◯ ◯

----------------------------------] ◯ ◯ ◯

----------------------------------] ◯ ◯ ◯

----------------------------------] ◯ ◯ ◯

NOTES:

Symptom Log

Description	MILD	MOD	SEVERE
------------------------------------]	◯	◯	◯
------------------------------------]	◯	◯	◯
------------------------------------]	◯	◯	◯
------------------------------------]	◯	◯	◯
------------------------------------]	◯	◯	◯
------------------------------------]	◯	◯	◯
------------------------------------]	◯	◯	◯
------------------------------------]	◯	◯	◯
------------------------------------]	◯	◯	◯
------------------------------------]	◯	◯	◯
------------------------------------]	◯	◯	◯

NOTES:

Symptom Log

Description   MILD   MOD   SEVERE

-----------------------------------] ◯ ◯ ◯

-----------------------------------] ◯ ◯ ◯

-----------------------------------] ◯ ◯ ◯

-----------------------------------] ◯ ◯ ◯

-----------------------------------] ◯ ◯ ◯

-----------------------------------] ◯ ◯ ◯

-----------------------------------] ◯ ◯ ◯

-----------------------------------] ◯ ◯ ◯

-----------------------------------] ◯ ◯ ◯

-----------------------------------] ◯ ◯ ◯

-----------------------------------] ◯ ◯ ◯

NOTES:

Symptom Log

Description	MILD	MOD	SEVERE
-------------------------------]	◯	◯	◯
-------------------------------]	◯	◯	◯
-------------------------------]	◯	◯	◯
-------------------------------]	◯	◯	◯
-------------------------------]	◯	◯	◯
-------------------------------]	◯	◯	◯
-------------------------------]	◯	◯	◯
-------------------------------]	◯	◯	◯
-------------------------------]	◯	◯	◯
-------------------------------]	◯	◯	◯
-------------------------------]	◯	◯	◯

NOTES:

Symptom Log

Description	MILD	MOD	SEVERE
----------------------------------]	◯	◯	◯
----------------------------------]	◯	◯	◯
----------------------------------]	◯	◯	◯
----------------------------------]	◯	◯	◯
----------------------------------]	◯	◯	◯
----------------------------------]	◯	◯	◯
----------------------------------]	◯	◯	◯
----------------------------------]	◯	◯	◯
----------------------------------]	◯	◯	◯
----------------------------------]	◯	◯	◯
----------------------------------]	◯	◯	◯

NOTES:

Symptom Log

Description   MILD   MOD   SEVERE

----------------------------------] ◯ ◯ ◯

----------------------------------] ◯ ◯ ◯

----------------------------------] ◯ ◯ ◯

----------------------------------] ◯ ◯ ◯

----------------------------------] ◯ ◯ ◯

----------------------------------] ◯ ◯ ◯

----------------------------------] ◯ ◯ ◯

----------------------------------] ◯ ◯ ◯

----------------------------------] ◯ ◯ ◯

----------------------------------] ◯ ◯ ◯

----------------------------------] ◯ ◯ ◯

NOTES:

Symptom Log

Description	MILD	MOD	SEVERE
------------------------------------]	◯	◯	◯
------------------------------------]	◯	◯	◯
------------------------------------]	◯	◯	◯
------------------------------------]	◯	◯	◯
------------------------------------]	◯	◯	◯
------------------------------------]	◯	◯	◯
------------------------------------]	◯	◯	◯
------------------------------------]	◯	◯	◯
------------------------------------]	◯	◯	◯
------------------------------------]	◯	◯	◯
------------------------------------]	◯	◯	◯

NOTES:

Symptom Log

Description	MILD	MOD	SEVERE
----------------------------------]	◯	◯	◯
----------------------------------]	◯	◯	◯
----------------------------------]	◯	◯	◯
----------------------------------]	◯	◯	◯
----------------------------------]	◯	◯	◯
----------------------------------]	◯	◯	◯
----------------------------------]	◯	◯	◯
----------------------------------]	◯	◯	◯
----------------------------------]	◯	◯	◯
----------------------------------]	◯	◯	◯
----------------------------------]	◯	◯	◯

NOTES:

Symptom Log

Description   MILD   MOD   SEVERE

-----------------------------------]   ◯   ◯   ◯

-----------------------------------]   ◯   ◯   ◯

-----------------------------------]   ◯   ◯   ◯

-----------------------------------]   ◯   ◯   ◯

-----------------------------------]   ◯   ◯   ◯

-----------------------------------]   ◯   ◯   ◯

-----------------------------------]   ◯   ◯   ◯

-----------------------------------]   ◯   ◯   ◯

-----------------------------------]   ◯   ◯   ◯

-----------------------------------]   ◯   ◯   ◯

-----------------------------------]   ◯   ◯   ◯

NOTES:

Symptom Log

Description	MILD	MOD	SEVERE
----------------------------------]	◯	◯	◯
----------------------------------]	◯	◯	◯
----------------------------------]	◯	◯	◯
----------------------------------]	◯	◯	◯
----------------------------------]	◯	◯	◯
----------------------------------]	◯	◯	◯
----------------------------------]	◯	◯	◯
----------------------------------]	◯	◯	◯
----------------------------------]	◯	◯	◯
----------------------------------]	◯	◯	◯
----------------------------------]	◯	◯	◯

NOTES:

Symptom Log

Description	MILD	MOD	SEVERE
-----------------------------------]	◯	◯	◯
-----------------------------------]	◯	◯	◯
-----------------------------------]	◯	◯	◯
-----------------------------------]	◯	◯	◯
-----------------------------------]	◯	◯	◯
-----------------------------------]	◯	◯	◯
-----------------------------------]	◯	◯	◯
-----------------------------------]	◯	◯	◯
-----------------------------------]	◯	◯	◯
-----------------------------------]	◯	◯	◯
-----------------------------------]	◯	◯	◯

NOTES:

Symptom Log

Description   MILD   MOD   SEVERE

Description	MILD	MOD	SEVERE
------------------------------]	◯	◯	◯
------------------------------]	◯	◯	◯
------------------------------]	◯	◯	◯
------------------------------]	◯	◯	◯
------------------------------]	◯	◯	◯
------------------------------]	◯	◯	◯
------------------------------]	◯	◯	◯
------------------------------]	◯	◯	◯
------------------------------]	◯	◯	◯
------------------------------]	◯	◯	◯
------------------------------]	◯	◯	◯

NOTES:

Symptom Log

Description	MILD	MOD	SEVERE
----------------------------------]	◯	◯	◯
----------------------------------]	◯	◯	◯
----------------------------------]	◯	◯	◯
----------------------------------]	◯	◯	◯
----------------------------------]	◯	◯	◯
----------------------------------]	◯	◯	◯
----------------------------------]	◯	◯	◯
----------------------------------]	◯	◯	◯
----------------------------------]	◯	◯	◯
----------------------------------]	◯	◯	◯
----------------------------------]	◯	◯	◯

NOTES:

Symptom Log

Description	MILD	MOD	SEVERE
------------------------------]	◯	◯	◯
------------------------------]	◯	◯	◯
------------------------------]	◯	◯	◯
------------------------------]	◯	◯	◯
------------------------------]	◯	◯	◯
------------------------------]	◯	◯	◯
------------------------------]	◯	◯	◯
------------------------------]	◯	◯	◯
------------------------------]	◯	◯	◯
------------------------------]	◯	◯	◯
------------------------------]	◯	◯	◯

NOTES:

Symptom Log

Description	MILD	MOD	SEVERE
----------------------------------]	◯	◯	◯
----------------------------------]	◯	◯	◯
----------------------------------]	◯	◯	◯
----------------------------------]	◯	◯	◯
----------------------------------]	◯	◯	◯
----------------------------------]	◯	◯	◯
----------------------------------]	◯	◯	◯
----------------------------------]	◯	◯	◯
----------------------------------]	◯	◯	◯
----------------------------------]	◯	◯	◯
----------------------------------]	◯	◯	◯

NOTES:

Symptom Log

Description   MILD   MOD   SEVERE

------------------------------------]   ◯   ◯   ◯

------------------------------------]   ◯   ◯   ◯

------------------------------------]   ◯   ◯   ◯

------------------------------------]   ◯   ◯   ◯

------------------------------------]   ◯   ◯   ◯

------------------------------------]   ◯   ◯   ◯

------------------------------------]   ◯   ◯   ◯

------------------------------------]   ◯   ◯   ◯

------------------------------------]   ◯   ◯   ◯

------------------------------------]   ◯   ◯   ◯

------------------------------------]   ◯   ◯   ◯

NOTES:

Symptom Log

Description	MILD	MOD	SEVERE
-------------------------------]	◯	◯	◯
-------------------------------]	◯	◯	◯
-------------------------------]	◯	◯	◯
-------------------------------]	◯	◯	◯
-------------------------------]	◯	◯	◯
-------------------------------]	◯	◯	◯
-------------------------------]	◯	◯	◯
-------------------------------]	◯	◯	◯
-------------------------------]	◯	◯	◯
-------------------------------]	◯	◯	◯
-------------------------------]	◯	◯	◯

NOTES:

Symptom Log

Description	MILD	MOD	SEVERE
-----------------------------------]	◯	◯	◯
-----------------------------------]	◯	◯	◯
-----------------------------------]	◯	◯	◯
-----------------------------------]	◯	◯	◯
-----------------------------------]	◯	◯	◯
-----------------------------------]	◯	◯	◯
-----------------------------------]	◯	◯	◯
-----------------------------------]	◯	◯	◯
-----------------------------------]	◯	◯	◯
-----------------------------------]	◯	◯	◯
-----------------------------------]	◯	◯	◯

NOTES:

Symptom Log

Description	MILD	MOD	SEVERE
------------------------------------]	○	○	○
------------------------------------]	○	○	○
------------------------------------]	○	○	○
------------------------------------]	○	○	○
------------------------------------]	○	○	○
------------------------------------]	○	○	○
------------------------------------]	○	○	○
------------------------------------]	○	○	○
------------------------------------]	○	○	○
------------------------------------]	○	○	○
------------------------------------]	○	○	○

NOTES:

Symptom Log

Description	MILD	MOD	SEVERE
------------------------------------]	◯	◯	◯
------------------------------------]	◯	◯	◯
------------------------------------]	◯	◯	◯
------------------------------------]	◯	◯	◯
------------------------------------]	◯	◯	◯
------------------------------------]	◯	◯	◯
------------------------------------]	◯	◯	◯
------------------------------------]	◯	◯	◯
------------------------------------]	◯	◯	◯
------------------------------------]	◯	◯	◯
------------------------------------]	◯	◯	◯

NOTES:

Symptom Log

Description	MILD	MOD	SEVERE
----------------------------------]	O	O	O
----------------------------------]	O	O	O
----------------------------------]	O	O	O
----------------------------------]	O	O	O
----------------------------------]	O	O	O
----------------------------------]	O	O	O
----------------------------------]	O	O	O
----------------------------------]	O	O	O
----------------------------------]	O	O	O
----------------------------------]	O	O	O
----------------------------------]	O	O	O

NOTES:

Symptom Log

Description	MILD	MOD	SEVERE
------------------------------------]	◯	◯	◯
------------------------------------]	◯	◯	◯
------------------------------------]	◯	◯	◯
------------------------------------]	◯	◯	◯
------------------------------------]	◯	◯	◯
------------------------------------]	◯	◯	◯
------------------------------------]	◯	◯	◯
------------------------------------]	◯	◯	◯
------------------------------------]	◯	◯	◯
------------------------------------]	◯	◯	◯
------------------------------------]	◯	◯	◯

NOTES:

Symptom Log

Description	MILD	MOD	SEVERE
------------------------------------]	◯	◯	◯
------------------------------------]	◯	◯	◯
------------------------------------]	◯	◯	◯
------------------------------------]	◯	◯	◯
------------------------------------]	◯	◯	◯
------------------------------------]	◯	◯	◯
------------------------------------]	◯	◯	◯
------------------------------------]	◯	◯	◯
------------------------------------]	◯	◯	◯
------------------------------------]	◯	◯	◯
------------------------------------]	◯	◯	◯

NOTES:

Symptom Log

Description	MILD	MOD	SEVERE
------------------------------]	○	○	○
------------------------------]	○	○	○
------------------------------]	○	○	○
------------------------------]	○	○	○
------------------------------]	○	○	○
------------------------------]	○	○	○
------------------------------]	○	○	○
------------------------------]	○	○	○
------------------------------]	○	○	○
------------------------------]	○	○	○
------------------------------]	○	○	○

NOTES:

Symptom Log

Description   MILD   MOD   SEVERE

-----------------------------------]   ◯   ◯   ◯

-----------------------------------]   ◯   ◯   ◯

-----------------------------------]   ◯   ◯   ◯

-----------------------------------]   ◯   ◯   ◯

-----------------------------------]   ◯   ◯   ◯

-----------------------------------]   ◯   ◯   ◯

-----------------------------------]   ◯   ◯   ◯

-----------------------------------]   ◯   ◯   ◯

-----------------------------------]   ◯   ◯   ◯

-----------------------------------]   ◯   ◯   ◯

-----------------------------------]   ◯   ◯   ◯

NOTES:

Symptom Log

Description   MILD   MOD   SEVERE

-----------------------------------] ◯   ◯   ◯

-----------------------------------] ◯   ◯   ◯

-----------------------------------] ◯   ◯   ◯

-----------------------------------] ◯   ◯   ◯

-----------------------------------] ◯   ◯   ◯

-----------------------------------] ◯   ◯   ◯

-----------------------------------] ◯   ◯   ◯

-----------------------------------] ◯   ◯   ◯

-----------------------------------] ◯   ◯   ◯

-----------------------------------] ◯   ◯   ◯

-----------------------------------] ◯   ◯   ◯

NOTES:

Symptom Log

Description	MILD	MOD	SEVERE
----------------------------------]	○	○	○
----------------------------------]	○	○	○
----------------------------------]	○	○	○
----------------------------------]	○	○	○
----------------------------------]	○	○	○
----------------------------------]	○	○	○
----------------------------------]	○	○	○
----------------------------------]	○	○	○
----------------------------------]	○	○	○
----------------------------------]	○	○	○
----------------------------------]	○	○	○

NOTES:

Symptom Log

Description	MILD	MOD	SEVERE
-----------------------------------]	◯	◯	◯
-----------------------------------]	◯	◯	◯
-----------------------------------]	◯	◯	◯
-----------------------------------]	◯	◯	◯
-----------------------------------]	◯	◯	◯
-----------------------------------]	◯	◯	◯
-----------------------------------]	◯	◯	◯
-----------------------------------]	◯	◯	◯
-----------------------------------]	◯	◯	◯
-----------------------------------]	◯	◯	◯
-----------------------------------]	◯	◯	◯

NOTES:

Symptom Log

Description	MILD	MOD	SEVERE
-----------------------------]	◯	◯	◯
-----------------------------]	◯	◯	◯
-----------------------------]	◯	◯	◯
-----------------------------]	◯	◯	◯
-----------------------------]	◯	◯	◯
-----------------------------]	◯	◯	◯
-----------------------------]	◯	◯	◯
-----------------------------]	◯	◯	◯
-----------------------------]	◯	◯	◯
-----------------------------]	◯	◯	◯
-----------------------------]	◯	◯	◯

NOTES:

Symptom Log

Description	MILD	MOD	SEVERE
------------------------------------]	◯	◯	◯
------------------------------------]	◯	◯	◯
------------------------------------]	◯	◯	◯
------------------------------------]	◯	◯	◯
------------------------------------]	◯	◯	◯
------------------------------------]	◯	◯	◯
------------------------------------]	◯	◯	◯
------------------------------------]	◯	◯	◯
------------------------------------]	◯	◯	◯
------------------------------------]	◯	◯	◯
------------------------------------]	◯	◯	◯

NOTES:

Symptom Log

Description	MILD	MOD	SEVERE
------------------------------------]	○	○	○
------------------------------------]	○	○	○
------------------------------------]	○	○	○
------------------------------------]	○	○	○
------------------------------------]	○	○	○
------------------------------------]	○	○	○
------------------------------------]	○	○	○
------------------------------------]	○	○	○
------------------------------------]	○	○	○
------------------------------------]	○	○	○
------------------------------------]	○	○	○

NOTES:

Symptom Log

Description	MILD	MOD	SEVERE
------------------------------------]	◯	◯	◯
------------------------------------]	◯	◯	◯
------------------------------------]	◯	◯	◯
------------------------------------]	◯	◯	◯
------------------------------------]	◯	◯	◯
------------------------------------]	◯	◯	◯
------------------------------------]	◯	◯	◯
------------------------------------]	◯	◯	◯
------------------------------------]	◯	◯	◯
------------------------------------]	◯	◯	◯
------------------------------------]	◯	◯	◯

NOTES:

Symptom Log

Description	MILD	MOD	SEVERE
----------------------------------]	◯	◯	◯
----------------------------------]	◯	◯	◯
----------------------------------]	◯	◯	◯
----------------------------------]	◯	◯	◯
----------------------------------]	◯	◯	◯
----------------------------------]	◯	◯	◯
----------------------------------]	◯	◯	◯
----------------------------------]	◯	◯	◯
----------------------------------]	◯	◯	◯
----------------------------------]	◯	◯	◯
----------------------------------]	◯	◯	◯

NOTES:

Symptom Log

Description	MILD	MOD	SEVERE
------------------------------]	◯	◯	◯
------------------------------]	◯	◯	◯
------------------------------]	◯	◯	◯
------------------------------]	◯	◯	◯
------------------------------]	◯	◯	◯
------------------------------]	◯	◯	◯
------------------------------]	◯	◯	◯
------------------------------]	◯	◯	◯
------------------------------]	◯	◯	◯
------------------------------]	◯	◯	◯
------------------------------]	◯	◯	◯

NOTES:

Symptom Log

Description	MILD	MOD	SEVERE
---------------------------------]	○	○	○
---------------------------------]	○	○	○
---------------------------------]	○	○	○
---------------------------------]	○	○	○
---------------------------------]	○	○	○
---------------------------------]	○	○	○
---------------------------------]	○	○	○
---------------------------------]	○	○	○
---------------------------------]	○	○	○
---------------------------------]	○	○	○
---------------------------------]	○	○	○

NOTES:

Symptom Log

Description	MILD	MOD	SEVERE
-----------------------------------]	◯	◯	◯
-----------------------------------]	◯	◯	◯
-----------------------------------]	◯	◯	◯
-----------------------------------]	◯	◯	◯
-----------------------------------]	◯	◯	◯
-----------------------------------]	◯	◯	◯
-----------------------------------]	◯	◯	◯
-----------------------------------]	◯	◯	◯
-----------------------------------]	◯	◯	◯
-----------------------------------]	◯	◯	◯
-----------------------------------]	◯	◯	◯

NOTES:

Symptom Log

Description	MILD	MOD	SEVERE
----------------------------------]	◯	◯	◯
----------------------------------]	◯	◯	◯
----------------------------------]	◯	◯	◯
----------------------------------]	◯	◯	◯
----------------------------------]	◯	◯	◯
----------------------------------]	◯	◯	◯
----------------------------------]	◯	◯	◯
----------------------------------]	◯	◯	◯
----------------------------------]	◯	◯	◯
----------------------------------]	◯	◯	◯
----------------------------------]	◯	◯	◯

NOTES:

Symptom Log

Description   MILD   MOD   SEVERE

-----------------------------------]   ◯   ◯   ◯

-----------------------------------]   ◯   ◯   ◯

-----------------------------------]   ◯   ◯   ◯

-----------------------------------]   ◯   ◯   ◯

-----------------------------------]   ◯   ◯   ◯

-----------------------------------]   ◯   ◯   ◯

-----------------------------------]   ◯   ◯   ◯

-----------------------------------]   ◯   ◯   ◯

-----------------------------------]   ◯   ◯   ◯

-----------------------------------]   ◯   ◯   ◯

-----------------------------------]   ◯   ◯   ◯

NOTES:

Symptom Log

Description	MILD	MOD	SEVERE
------------------------------------]	◯	◯	◯
------------------------------------]	◯	◯	◯
------------------------------------]	◯	◯	◯
------------------------------------]	◯	◯	◯
------------------------------------]	◯	◯	◯
------------------------------------]	◯	◯	◯
------------------------------------]	◯	◯	◯
------------------------------------]	◯	◯	◯
------------------------------------]	◯	◯	◯
------------------------------------]	◯	◯	◯
------------------------------------]	◯	◯	◯

NOTES:

I can & I will

You are strong and fearless.

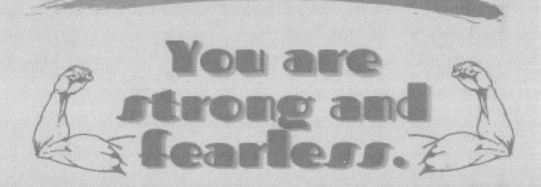

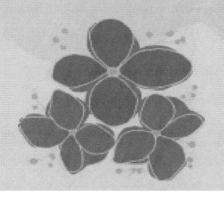

Symptom Log

Description	MILD	MOD	SEVERE
----------------------------------]	◯	◯	◯
----------------------------------]	◯	◯	◯
----------------------------------]	◯	◯	◯
----------------------------------]	◯	◯	◯
----------------------------------]	◯	◯	◯
----------------------------------]	◯	◯	◯
----------------------------------]	◯	◯	◯
----------------------------------]	◯	◯	◯
----------------------------------]	◯	◯	◯
----------------------------------]	◯	◯	◯
----------------------------------]	◯	◯	◯

NOTES:

Symptom Log

Description	MILD	MOD	SEVERE
--------------------------------]	◯	◯	◯
--------------------------------]	◯	◯	◯
--------------------------------]	◯	◯	◯
--------------------------------]	◯	◯	◯
--------------------------------]	◯	◯	◯
--------------------------------]	◯	◯	◯
--------------------------------]	◯	◯	◯
--------------------------------]	◯	◯	◯
--------------------------------]	◯	◯	◯
--------------------------------]	◯	◯	◯
--------------------------------]	◯	◯	◯

NOTES:

Symptom Log

Description	MILD	MOD	SEVERE
------------------------------------]	◯	◯	◯
------------------------------------]	◯	◯	◯
------------------------------------]	◯	◯	◯
------------------------------------]	◯	◯	◯
------------------------------------]	◯	◯	◯
------------------------------------]	◯	◯	◯
------------------------------------]	◯	◯	◯
------------------------------------]	◯	◯	◯
------------------------------------]	◯	◯	◯
------------------------------------]	◯	◯	◯
------------------------------------]	◯	◯	◯

NOTES:

Symptom Log

Description	MILD	MOD	SEVERE
---------------------------------]	◯	◯	◯
---------------------------------]	◯	◯	◯
---------------------------------]	◯	◯	◯
---------------------------------]	◯	◯	◯
---------------------------------]	◯	◯	◯
---------------------------------]	◯	◯	◯
---------------------------------]	◯	◯	◯
---------------------------------]	◯	◯	◯
---------------------------------]	◯	◯	◯
---------------------------------]	◯	◯	◯
---------------------------------]	◯	◯	◯

NOTES:

Symptom Log

Description	MILD	MOD	SEVERE
-----------------------------------]	◯	◯	◯
-----------------------------------]	◯	◯	◯
-----------------------------------]	◯	◯	◯
-----------------------------------]	◯	◯	◯
-----------------------------------]	◯	◯	◯
-----------------------------------]	◯	◯	◯
-----------------------------------]	◯	◯	◯
-----------------------------------]	◯	◯	◯
-----------------------------------]	◯	◯	◯
-----------------------------------]	◯	◯	◯
-----------------------------------]	◯	◯	◯

NOTES:

Symptom Log

Description	MILD	MOD	SEVERE
--------------------------------]	○	○	○
--------------------------------]	○	○	○
--------------------------------]	○	○	○
--------------------------------]	○	○	○
--------------------------------]	○	○	○
--------------------------------]	○	○	○
--------------------------------]	○	○	○
--------------------------------]	○	○	○
--------------------------------]	○	○	○
--------------------------------]	○	○	○
--------------------------------]	○	○	○

NOTES:

Symptom Log

Description   MILD   MOD   SEVERE

-----------------------------------]   ◯   ◯   ◯

-----------------------------------]   ◯   ◯   ◯

-----------------------------------]   ◯   ◯   ◯

-----------------------------------]   ◯   ◯   ◯

-----------------------------------]   ◯   ◯   ◯

-----------------------------------]   ◯   ◯   ◯

-----------------------------------]   ◯   ◯   ◯

-----------------------------------]   ◯   ◯   ◯

-----------------------------------]   ◯   ◯   ◯

-----------------------------------]   ◯   ◯   ◯

-----------------------------------]   ◯   ◯   ◯

NOTES:

Symptom Log

Description	MILD	MOD	SEVERE
------------------------------------]	◯	◯	◯
------------------------------------]	◯	◯	◯
------------------------------------]	◯	◯	◯
------------------------------------]	◯	◯	◯
------------------------------------]	◯	◯	◯
------------------------------------]	◯	◯	◯
------------------------------------]	◯	◯	◯
------------------------------------]	◯	◯	◯
------------------------------------]	◯	◯	◯
------------------------------------]	◯	◯	◯
------------------------------------]	◯	◯	◯

NOTES:

Symptom Log

Description	MILD	MOD	SEVERE
----------------------------------]	◯	◯	◯
----------------------------------]	◯	◯	◯
----------------------------------]	◯	◯	◯
----------------------------------]	◯	◯	◯
----------------------------------]	◯	◯	◯
----------------------------------]	◯	◯	◯
----------------------------------]	◯	◯	◯
----------------------------------]	◯	◯	◯
----------------------------------]	◯	◯	◯
----------------------------------]	◯	◯	◯
----------------------------------]	◯	◯	◯

NOTES:

Symptom Log

Description	MILD	MOD	SEVERE
------------------------------------]	◯	◯	◯
------------------------------------]	◯	◯	◯
------------------------------------]	◯	◯	◯
------------------------------------]	◯	◯	◯
------------------------------------]	◯	◯	◯
------------------------------------]	◯	◯	◯
------------------------------------]	◯	◯	◯
------------------------------------]	◯	◯	◯
------------------------------------]	◯	◯	◯
------------------------------------]	◯	◯	◯
------------------------------------]	◯	◯	◯

NOTES:

Symptom Log

Description	MILD	MOD	SEVERE
------------------------------------]	◯	◯	◯
------------------------------------]	◯	◯	◯
------------------------------------]	◯	◯	◯
------------------------------------]	◯	◯	◯
------------------------------------]	◯	◯	◯
------------------------------------]	◯	◯	◯
------------------------------------]	◯	◯	◯
------------------------------------]	◯	◯	◯
------------------------------------]	◯	◯	◯
------------------------------------]	◯	◯	◯
------------------------------------]	◯	◯	◯

NOTES:

Symptom Log

Description	MILD	MOD	SEVERE
-------------------------------------]	◯	◯	◯
-------------------------------------]	◯	◯	◯
-------------------------------------]	◯	◯	◯
-------------------------------------]	◯	◯	◯
-------------------------------------]	◯	◯	◯
-------------------------------------]	◯	◯	◯
-------------------------------------]	◯	◯	◯
-------------------------------------]	◯	◯	◯
-------------------------------------]	◯	◯	◯
-------------------------------------]	◯	◯	◯
-------------------------------------]	◯	◯	◯

NOTES:

Symptom Log

Description	MILD	MOD	SEVERE
----------------------------------]	○	○	○
----------------------------------]	○	○	○
----------------------------------]	○	○	○
----------------------------------]	○	○	○
----------------------------------]	○	○	○
----------------------------------]	○	○	○
----------------------------------]	○	○	○
----------------------------------]	○	○	○
----------------------------------]	○	○	○
----------------------------------]	○	○	○
----------------------------------]	○	○	○

NOTES:

Symptom Log

Description   MILD   MOD   SEVERE

-----------------------------------]   ◯   ◯   ◯

-----------------------------------]   ◯   ◯   ◯

-----------------------------------]   ◯   ◯   ◯

-----------------------------------]   ◯   ◯   ◯

-----------------------------------]   ◯   ◯   ◯

-----------------------------------]   ◯   ◯   ◯

-----------------------------------]   ◯   ◯   ◯

-----------------------------------]   ◯   ◯   ◯

-----------------------------------]   ◯   ◯   ◯

-----------------------------------]   ◯   ◯   ◯

-----------------------------------]   ◯   ◯   ◯

NOTES:

Symptom Log

Description	MILD	MOD	SEVERE
--]	○	○	○
--]	○	○	○
--]	○	○	○
--]	○	○	○
--]	○	○	○
--]	○	○	○
--]	○	○	○
--]	○	○	○
--]	○	○	○
--]	○	○	○
--]	○	○	○

NOTES:

Symptom Log

Description	MILD	MOD	SEVERE
-------------------------------]	◯	◯	◯
-------------------------------]	◯	◯	◯
-------------------------------]	◯	◯	◯
-------------------------------]	◯	◯	◯
-------------------------------]	◯	◯	◯
-------------------------------]	◯	◯	◯
-------------------------------]	◯	◯	◯
-------------------------------]	◯	◯	◯
-------------------------------]	◯	◯	◯
-------------------------------]	◯	◯	◯
-------------------------------]	◯	◯	◯

NOTES:

Symptom Log

Description	MILD	MOD	SEVERE
------------------------------]	◯	◯	◯
------------------------------]	◯	◯	◯
------------------------------]	◯	◯	◯
------------------------------]	◯	◯	◯
------------------------------]	◯	◯	◯
------------------------------]	◯	◯	◯
------------------------------]	◯	◯	◯
------------------------------]	◯	◯	◯
------------------------------]	◯	◯	◯
------------------------------]	◯	◯	◯
------------------------------]	◯	◯	◯

NOTES:

Symptom Log

Description   MILD   MOD   SEVERE

----------------------------------] ◯ ◯ ◯

----------------------------------] ◯ ◯ ◯

----------------------------------] ◯ ◯ ◯

----------------------------------] ◯ ◯ ◯

----------------------------------] ◯ ◯ ◯

----------------------------------] ◯ ◯ ◯

----------------------------------] ◯ ◯ ◯

----------------------------------] ◯ ◯ ◯

----------------------------------] ◯ ◯ ◯

----------------------------------] ◯ ◯ ◯

----------------------------------] ◯ ◯ ◯

NOTES:

Symptom Log

Description	MILD	MOD	SEVERE
----------------------------------]	◯	◯	◯
----------------------------------]	◯	◯	◯
----------------------------------]	◯	◯	◯
----------------------------------]	◯	◯	◯
----------------------------------]	◯	◯	◯
----------------------------------]	◯	◯	◯
----------------------------------]	◯	◯	◯
----------------------------------]	◯	◯	◯
----------------------------------]	◯	◯	◯
----------------------------------]	◯	◯	◯
----------------------------------]	◯	◯	◯

NOTES:

Symptom Log

Description   MILD   MOD   SEVERE

-------------------------------------] ◯   ◯   ◯

-------------------------------------] ◯   ◯   ◯

-------------------------------------] ◯   ◯   ◯

-------------------------------------] ◯   ◯   ◯

-------------------------------------] ◯   ◯   ◯

-------------------------------------] ◯   ◯   ◯

-------------------------------------] ◯   ◯   ◯

-------------------------------------] ◯   ◯   ◯

-------------------------------------] ◯   ◯   ◯

-------------------------------------] ◯   ◯   ◯

-------------------------------------] ◯   ◯   ◯

NOTES:

Symptom Log

Description	MILD	MOD	SEVERE
-----------------------------------]	◯	◯	◯
-----------------------------------]	◯	◯	◯
-----------------------------------]	◯	◯	◯
-----------------------------------]	◯	◯	◯
-----------------------------------]	◯	◯	◯
-----------------------------------]	◯	◯	◯
-----------------------------------]	◯	◯	◯
-----------------------------------]	◯	◯	◯
-----------------------------------]	◯	◯	◯
-----------------------------------]	◯	◯	◯
-----------------------------------]	◯	◯	◯

NOTES:

Symptom Log

Description   MILD   MOD   SEVERE

-------------------------------------] ◯ ◯ ◯

-------------------------------------] ◯ ◯ ◯

-------------------------------------] ◯ ◯ ◯

-------------------------------------] ◯ ◯ ◯

-------------------------------------] ◯ ◯ ◯

-------------------------------------] ◯ ◯ ◯

-------------------------------------] ◯ ◯ ◯

-------------------------------------] ◯ ◯ ◯

-------------------------------------] ◯ ◯ ◯

-------------------------------------] ◯ ◯ ◯

-------------------------------------] ◯ ◯ ◯

NOTES:

Symptom Log

Description	MILD	MOD	SEVERE
----------------------------------]	◯	◯	◯
----------------------------------]	◯	◯	◯
----------------------------------]	◯	◯	◯
----------------------------------]	◯	◯	◯
----------------------------------]	◯	◯	◯
----------------------------------]	◯	◯	◯
----------------------------------]	◯	◯	◯
----------------------------------]	◯	◯	◯
----------------------------------]	◯	◯	◯
----------------------------------]	◯	◯	◯
----------------------------------]	◯	◯	◯

NOTES:

Symptom Log

Description	MILD	MOD	SEVERE
-----------------------------------]	◯	◯	◯
-----------------------------------]	◯	◯	◯
-----------------------------------]	◯	◯	◯
-----------------------------------]	◯	◯	◯
-----------------------------------]	◯	◯	◯
-----------------------------------]	◯	◯	◯
-----------------------------------]	◯	◯	◯
-----------------------------------]	◯	◯	◯
-----------------------------------]	◯	◯	◯
-----------------------------------]	◯	◯	◯
-----------------------------------]	◯	◯	◯

NOTES:

Symptom Log

Description	MILD	MOD	SEVERE
------------------------------------]	◯	◯	◯
------------------------------------]	◯	◯	◯
------------------------------------]	◯	◯	◯
------------------------------------]	◯	◯	◯
------------------------------------]	◯	◯	◯
------------------------------------]	◯	◯	◯
------------------------------------]	◯	◯	◯
------------------------------------]	◯	◯	◯
------------------------------------]	◯	◯	◯
------------------------------------]	◯	◯	◯
------------------------------------]	◯	◯	◯

NOTES:

Symptom Log

Description	MILD	MOD	SEVERE
-------------------------------]	◯	◯	◯
-------------------------------]	◯	◯	◯
-------------------------------]	◯	◯	◯
-------------------------------]	◯	◯	◯
-------------------------------]	◯	◯	◯
-------------------------------]	◯	◯	◯
-------------------------------]	◯	◯	◯
-------------------------------]	◯	◯	◯
-------------------------------]	◯	◯	◯
-------------------------------]	◯	◯	◯
-------------------------------]	◯	◯	◯

NOTES:

Symptom Log

Description   MILD   MOD   SEVERE

-------------------------------------] ◯ ◯ ◯

-------------------------------------] ◯ ◯ ◯

-------------------------------------] ◯ ◯ ◯

-------------------------------------] ◯ ◯ ◯

-------------------------------------] ◯ ◯ ◯

-------------------------------------] ◯ ◯ ◯

-------------------------------------] ◯ ◯ ◯

-------------------------------------] ◯ ◯ ◯

-------------------------------------] ◯ ◯ ◯

-------------------------------------] ◯ ◯ ◯

-------------------------------------] ◯ ◯ ◯

NOTES:

Symptom Log

Description	MILD	MOD	SEVERE
-------------------------------]	◯	◯	◯
-------------------------------]	◯	◯	◯
-------------------------------]	◯	◯	◯
-------------------------------]	◯	◯	◯
-------------------------------]	◯	◯	◯
-------------------------------]	◯	◯	◯
-------------------------------]	◯	◯	◯
-------------------------------]	◯	◯	◯
-------------------------------]	◯	◯	◯
-------------------------------]	◯	◯	◯
-------------------------------]	◯	◯	◯

NOTES:

Symptom Log

Description	MILD	MOD	SEVERE
------------------------------------]	◯	◯	◯
------------------------------------]	◯	◯	◯
------------------------------------]	◯	◯	◯
------------------------------------]	◯	◯	◯
------------------------------------]	◯	◯	◯
------------------------------------]	◯	◯	◯
------------------------------------]	◯	◯	◯
------------------------------------]	◯	◯	◯
------------------------------------]	◯	◯	◯
------------------------------------]	◯	◯	◯
------------------------------------]	◯	◯	◯

NOTES:

Symptom Log

Description	MILD	MOD	SEVERE
----------------------------------]	○	○	○
----------------------------------]	○	○	○
----------------------------------]	○	○	○
----------------------------------]	○	○	○
----------------------------------]	○	○	○
----------------------------------]	○	○	○
----------------------------------]	○	○	○
----------------------------------]	○	○	○
----------------------------------]	○	○	○
----------------------------------]	○	○	○
----------------------------------]	○	○	○

NOTES:

Symptom Log

Description   MILD   MOD   SEVERE

--] ◯ ◯ ◯

--] ◯ ◯ ◯

--] ◯ ◯ ◯

--] ◯ ◯ ◯

--] ◯ ◯ ◯

--] ◯ ◯ ◯

--] ◯ ◯ ◯

--] ◯ ◯ ◯

--] ◯ ◯ ◯

--] ◯ ◯ ◯

--] ◯ ◯ ◯

NOTES:

Symptom Log

Description   MILD   MOD   SEVERE

---------------------------------] ◯ ◯ ◯

---------------------------------] ◯ ◯ ◯

---------------------------------] ◯ ◯ ◯

---------------------------------] ◯ ◯ ◯

---------------------------------] ◯ ◯ ◯

---------------------------------] ◯ ◯ ◯

---------------------------------] ◯ ◯ ◯

---------------------------------] ◯ ◯ ◯

---------------------------------] ◯ ◯ ◯

---------------------------------] ◯ ◯ ◯

---------------------------------] ◯ ◯ ◯

NOTES:

Symptom Log

Description	MILD	MOD	SEVERE
----------------------------------]	◯	◯	◯
----------------------------------]	◯	◯	◯
----------------------------------]	◯	◯	◯
----------------------------------]	◯	◯	◯
----------------------------------]	◯	◯	◯
----------------------------------]	◯	◯	◯
----------------------------------]	◯	◯	◯
----------------------------------]	◯	◯	◯
----------------------------------]	◯	◯	◯
----------------------------------]	◯	◯	◯
----------------------------------]	◯	◯	◯

NOTES:

Symptom Log

Description	MILD	MOD	SEVERE
-------------------------------]	○	○	○
-------------------------------]	○	○	○
-------------------------------]	○	○	○
-------------------------------]	○	○	○
-------------------------------]	○	○	○
-------------------------------]	○	○	○
-------------------------------]	○	○	○
-------------------------------]	○	○	○
-------------------------------]	○	○	○
-------------------------------]	○	○	○
-------------------------------]	○	○	○

NOTES:

Symptom Log

Description	MILD	MOD	SEVERE
-------------------------------------]	◯	◯	◯
-------------------------------------]	◯	◯	◯
-------------------------------------]	◯	◯	◯
-------------------------------------]	◯	◯	◯
-------------------------------------]	◯	◯	◯
-------------------------------------]	◯	◯	◯
-------------------------------------]	◯	◯	◯
-------------------------------------]	◯	◯	◯
-------------------------------------]	◯	◯	◯
-------------------------------------]	◯	◯	◯
-------------------------------------]	◯	◯	◯

NOTES:

Symptom Log

Description   MILD   MOD   SEVERE

------------------------------------] ◯ ◯ ◯

------------------------------------] ◯ ◯ ◯

------------------------------------] ◯ ◯ ◯

------------------------------------] ◯ ◯ ◯

------------------------------------] ◯ ◯ ◯

------------------------------------] ◯ ◯ ◯

------------------------------------] ◯ ◯ ◯

------------------------------------] ◯ ◯ ◯

------------------------------------] ◯ ◯ ◯

------------------------------------] ◯ ◯ ◯

------------------------------------] ◯ ◯ ◯

NOTES:

Symptom Log

Description	MILD	MOD	SEVERE
------------------------------------]	◯	◯	◯
------------------------------------]	◯	◯	◯
------------------------------------]	◯	◯	◯
------------------------------------]	◯	◯	◯
------------------------------------]	◯	◯	◯
------------------------------------]	◯	◯	◯
------------------------------------]	◯	◯	◯
------------------------------------]	◯	◯	◯
------------------------------------]	◯	◯	◯
------------------------------------]	◯	◯	◯
------------------------------------]	◯	◯	◯

NOTES:

Symptom Log

Description	MILD	MOD	SEVERE
------------------------------------]	◯	◯	◯
------------------------------------]	◯	◯	◯
------------------------------------]	◯	◯	◯
------------------------------------]	◯	◯	◯
------------------------------------]	◯	◯	◯
------------------------------------]	◯	◯	◯
------------------------------------]	◯	◯	◯
------------------------------------]	◯	◯	◯
------------------------------------]	◯	◯	◯
------------------------------------]	◯	◯	◯
------------------------------------]	◯	◯	◯

NOTES:

Symptom Log

Description	MILD	MOD	SEVERE
----------------------------------]	◯	◯	◯
----------------------------------]	◯	◯	◯
----------------------------------]	◯	◯	◯
----------------------------------]	◯	◯	◯
----------------------------------]	◯	◯	◯
----------------------------------]	◯	◯	◯
----------------------------------]	◯	◯	◯
----------------------------------]	◯	◯	◯
----------------------------------]	◯	◯	◯
----------------------------------]	◯	◯	◯
----------------------------------]	◯	◯	◯

NOTES:

Symptom Log

Description	MILD	MOD	SEVERE
---------------------------------]	◯	◯	◯
---------------------------------]	◯	◯	◯
---------------------------------]	◯	◯	◯
---------------------------------]	◯	◯	◯
---------------------------------]	◯	◯	◯
---------------------------------]	◯	◯	◯
---------------------------------]	◯	◯	◯
---------------------------------]	◯	◯	◯
---------------------------------]	◯	◯	◯
---------------------------------]	◯	◯	◯
---------------------------------]	◯	◯	◯

NOTES:

Symptom Log

Description　　　　　　　　MILD　　　MOD　　SEVERE

------------------------------------]　○　○　○

------------------------------------]　○　○　○

------------------------------------]　○　○　○

------------------------------------]　○　○　○

------------------------------------]　○　○　○

------------------------------------]　○　○　○

------------------------------------]　○　○　○

------------------------------------]　○　○　○

------------------------------------]　○　○　○

------------------------------------]　○　○　○

------------------------------------]　○　○　○

NOTES:

Symptom Log

Description	MILD	MOD	SEVERE
------------------------------]	◯	◯	◯
------------------------------]	◯	◯	◯
------------------------------]	◯	◯	◯
------------------------------]	◯	◯	◯
------------------------------]	◯	◯	◯
------------------------------]	◯	◯	◯
------------------------------]	◯	◯	◯
------------------------------]	◯	◯	◯
------------------------------]	◯	◯	◯
------------------------------]	◯	◯	◯
------------------------------]	◯	◯	◯

NOTES:

Symptom Log

Description	MILD	MOD	SEVERE
----------------------------------]	◯	◯	◯
----------------------------------]	◯	◯	◯
----------------------------------]	◯	◯	◯
----------------------------------]	◯	◯	◯
----------------------------------]	◯	◯	◯
----------------------------------]	◯	◯	◯
----------------------------------]	◯	◯	◯
----------------------------------]	◯	◯	◯
----------------------------------]	◯	◯	◯
----------------------------------]	◯	◯	◯
----------------------------------]	◯	◯	◯

NOTES:

Symptom Log

Description	MILD	MOD	SEVERE
----------------------------]	◯	◯	◯
----------------------------]	◯	◯	◯
----------------------------]	◯	◯	◯
----------------------------]	◯	◯	◯
----------------------------]	◯	◯	◯
----------------------------]	◯	◯	◯
----------------------------]	◯	◯	◯
----------------------------]	◯	◯	◯
----------------------------]	◯	◯	◯
----------------------------]	◯	◯	◯
----------------------------]	◯	◯	◯

NOTES:

Symptom Log

Description	MILD	MOD	SEVERE
-------------------------------]	◯	◯	◯
-------------------------------]	◯	◯	◯
-------------------------------]	◯	◯	◯
-------------------------------]	◯	◯	◯
-------------------------------]	◯	◯	◯
-------------------------------]	◯	◯	◯
-------------------------------]	◯	◯	◯
-------------------------------]	◯	◯	◯
-------------------------------]	◯	◯	◯
-------------------------------]	◯	◯	◯
-------------------------------]	◯	◯	◯

NOTES:

Symptom Log

Description	MILD	MOD	SEVERE
----------------------------------]	◯	◯	◯
----------------------------------]	◯	◯	◯
----------------------------------]	◯	◯	◯
----------------------------------]	◯	◯	◯
----------------------------------]	◯	◯	◯
----------------------------------]	◯	◯	◯
----------------------------------]	◯	◯	◯
----------------------------------]	◯	◯	◯
----------------------------------]	◯	◯	◯
----------------------------------]	◯	◯	◯
----------------------------------]	◯	◯	◯

NOTES:

Symptom Log

Description	MILD	MOD	SEVERE
----------------------------------]	◯	◯	◯
----------------------------------]	◯	◯	◯
----------------------------------]	◯	◯	◯
----------------------------------]	◯	◯	◯
----------------------------------]	◯	◯	◯
----------------------------------]	◯	◯	◯
----------------------------------]	◯	◯	◯
----------------------------------]	◯	◯	◯
----------------------------------]	◯	◯	◯
----------------------------------]	◯	◯	◯
----------------------------------]	◯	◯	◯

NOTES:

Symptom Log

Description   MILD   MOD   SEVERE

--------------------------------------]   ◯   ◯   ◯

--------------------------------------]   ◯   ◯   ◯

--------------------------------------]   ◯   ◯   ◯

--------------------------------------]   ◯   ◯   ◯

--------------------------------------]   ◯   ◯   ◯

--------------------------------------]   ◯   ◯   ◯

--------------------------------------]   ◯   ◯   ◯

--------------------------------------]   ◯   ◯   ◯

--------------------------------------]   ◯   ◯   ◯

--------------------------------------]   ◯   ◯   ◯

--------------------------------------]   ◯   ◯   ◯

NOTES:

Symptom Log

Description	MILD	MOD	SEVERE
------------------------------------]	◯	◯	◯
------------------------------------]	◯	◯	◯
------------------------------------]	◯	◯	◯
------------------------------------]	◯	◯	◯
------------------------------------]	◯	◯	◯
------------------------------------]	◯	◯	◯
------------------------------------]	◯	◯	◯
------------------------------------]	◯	◯	◯
------------------------------------]	◯	◯	◯
------------------------------------]	◯	◯	◯
------------------------------------]	◯	◯	◯

NOTES:

Symptom Log

Description	MILD	MOD	SEVERE
--]	◯	◯	◯
--]	◯	◯	◯
--]	◯	◯	◯
--]	◯	◯	◯
--]	◯	◯	◯
--]	◯	◯	◯
--]	◯	◯	◯
--]	◯	◯	◯
--]	◯	◯	◯
--]	◯	◯	◯
--]	◯	◯	◯

NOTES:

Symptom Log

Description	MILD	MOD	SEVERE
--------------------------------]	○	○	○
--------------------------------]	○	○	○
--------------------------------]	○	○	○
--------------------------------]	○	○	○
--------------------------------]	○	○	○
--------------------------------]	○	○	○
--------------------------------]	○	○	○
--------------------------------]	○	○	○
--------------------------------]	○	○	○
--------------------------------]	○	○	○
--------------------------------]	○	○	○

NOTES:

Symptom Log

Description	MILD	MOD	SEVERE
--------------------------------------]	◯	◯	◯
--------------------------------------]	◯	◯	◯
--------------------------------------]	◯	◯	◯
--------------------------------------]	◯	◯	◯
--------------------------------------]	◯	◯	◯
--------------------------------------]	◯	◯	◯
--------------------------------------]	◯	◯	◯
--------------------------------------]	◯	◯	◯
--------------------------------------]	◯	◯	◯
--------------------------------------]	◯	◯	◯
--------------------------------------]	◯	◯	◯

NOTES:

Symptom Log

Description	MILD	MOD	SEVERE
----------------------------------]	◯	◯	◯
----------------------------------]	◯	◯	◯
----------------------------------]	◯	◯	◯
----------------------------------]	◯	◯	◯
----------------------------------]	◯	◯	◯
----------------------------------]	◯	◯	◯
----------------------------------]	◯	◯	◯
----------------------------------]	◯	◯	◯
----------------------------------]	◯	◯	◯
----------------------------------]	◯	◯	◯
----------------------------------]	◯	◯	◯

NOTES:

Symptom Log

Description	MILD	MOD	SEVERE
--]	◯	◯	◯
--]	◯	◯	◯
--]	◯	◯	◯
--]	◯	◯	◯
--]	◯	◯	◯
--]	◯	◯	◯
--]	◯	◯	◯
--]	◯	◯	◯
--]	◯	◯	◯
--]	◯	◯	◯
--]	◯	◯	◯

NOTES:

Symptom Log

Description	MILD	MOD	SEVERE
----------------------------------]	◯	◯	◯
----------------------------------]	◯	◯	◯
----------------------------------]	◯	◯	◯
----------------------------------]	◯	◯	◯
----------------------------------]	◯	◯	◯
----------------------------------]	◯	◯	◯
----------------------------------]	◯	◯	◯
----------------------------------]	◯	◯	◯
----------------------------------]	◯	◯	◯
----------------------------------]	◯	◯	◯
----------------------------------]	◯	◯	◯

NOTES:

Symptom Log

Description	MILD	MOD	SEVERE
--------------------------------------]	◯	◯	◯
--------------------------------------]	◯	◯	◯
--------------------------------------]	◯	◯	◯
--------------------------------------]	◯	◯	◯
--------------------------------------]	◯	◯	◯
--------------------------------------]	◯	◯	◯
--------------------------------------]	◯	◯	◯
--------------------------------------]	◯	◯	◯
--------------------------------------]	◯	◯	◯
--------------------------------------]	◯	◯	◯
--------------------------------------]	◯	◯	◯

NOTES:

Symptom Log

Description	MILD	MOD	SEVERE
----------------------------------]	◯	◯	◯
----------------------------------]	◯	◯	◯
----------------------------------]	◯	◯	◯
----------------------------------]	◯	◯	◯
----------------------------------]	◯	◯	◯
----------------------------------]	◯	◯	◯
----------------------------------]	◯	◯	◯
----------------------------------]	◯	◯	◯
----------------------------------]	◯	◯	◯
----------------------------------]	◯	◯	◯
----------------------------------]	◯	◯	◯

NOTES:

Symptom Log

Description	MILD	MOD	SEVERE
--------------------------------]	◯	◯	◯
--------------------------------]	◯	◯	◯
--------------------------------]	◯	◯	◯
--------------------------------]	◯	◯	◯
--------------------------------]	◯	◯	◯
--------------------------------]	◯	◯	◯
--------------------------------]	◯	◯	◯
--------------------------------]	◯	◯	◯
--------------------------------]	◯	◯	◯
--------------------------------]	◯	◯	◯
--------------------------------]	◯	◯	◯

NOTES:

Symptom Log

Description	MILD	MOD	SEVERE
------------------------------]	◯	◯	◯
------------------------------]	◯	◯	◯
------------------------------]	◯	◯	◯
------------------------------]	◯	◯	◯
------------------------------]	◯	◯	◯
------------------------------]	◯	◯	◯
------------------------------]	◯	◯	◯
------------------------------]	◯	◯	◯
------------------------------]	◯	◯	◯
------------------------------]	◯	◯	◯
------------------------------]	◯	◯	◯

NOTES:

Symptom Log

Description	MILD	MOD	SEVERE
------------------------------------]	◯	◯	◯
------------------------------------]	◯	◯	◯
------------------------------------]	◯	◯	◯
------------------------------------]	◯	◯	◯
------------------------------------]	◯	◯	◯
------------------------------------]	◯	◯	◯
------------------------------------]	◯	◯	◯
------------------------------------]	◯	◯	◯
------------------------------------]	◯	◯	◯
------------------------------------]	◯	◯	◯
------------------------------------]	◯	◯	◯

NOTES:

Symptom Log

Description	MILD	MOD	SEVERE
------------------------------------]	◯	◯	◯
------------------------------------]	◯	◯	◯
------------------------------------]	◯	◯	◯
------------------------------------]	◯	◯	◯
------------------------------------]	◯	◯	◯
------------------------------------]	◯	◯	◯
------------------------------------]	◯	◯	◯
------------------------------------]	◯	◯	◯
------------------------------------]	◯	◯	◯
------------------------------------]	◯	◯	◯
------------------------------------]	◯	◯	◯

NOTES:

Symptom Log

Description	MILD	MOD	SEVERE
------------------------------]	◯	◯	◯
------------------------------]	◯	◯	◯
------------------------------]	◯	◯	◯
------------------------------]	◯	◯	◯
------------------------------]	◯	◯	◯
------------------------------]	◯	◯	◯
------------------------------]	◯	◯	◯
------------------------------]	◯	◯	◯
------------------------------]	◯	◯	◯
------------------------------]	◯	◯	◯
------------------------------]	◯	◯	◯

NOTES:

Symptom Log

Description	MILD	MOD	SEVERE
------------------------------]	◯	◯	◯
------------------------------]	◯	◯	◯
------------------------------]	◯	◯	◯
------------------------------]	◯	◯	◯
------------------------------]	◯	◯	◯
------------------------------]	◯	◯	◯
------------------------------]	◯	◯	◯
------------------------------]	◯	◯	◯
------------------------------]	◯	◯	◯
------------------------------]	◯	◯	◯
------------------------------]	◯	◯	◯

NOTES:

Symptom Log

Description	MILD	MOD	SEVERE
------------------------------]	◯	◯	◯
------------------------------]	◯	◯	◯
------------------------------]	◯	◯	◯
------------------------------]	◯	◯	◯
------------------------------]	◯	◯	◯
------------------------------]	◯	◯	◯
------------------------------]	◯	◯	◯
------------------------------]	◯	◯	◯
------------------------------]	◯	◯	◯
------------------------------]	◯	◯	◯
------------------------------]	◯	◯	◯

NOTES:

Symptom Log

Description   MILD   MOD   SEVERE

--------------------------------]   ◯   ◯   ◯

--------------------------------]   ◯   ◯   ◯

--------------------------------]   ◯   ◯   ◯

--------------------------------]   ◯   ◯   ◯

--------------------------------]   ◯   ◯   ◯

--------------------------------]   ◯   ◯   ◯

--------------------------------]   ◯   ◯   ◯

--------------------------------]   ◯   ◯   ◯

--------------------------------]   ◯   ◯   ◯

--------------------------------]   ◯   ◯   ◯

--------------------------------]   ◯   ◯   ◯

NOTES:

Symptom Log

Description	MILD	MOD	SEVERE
------------------------------------]	◯	◯	◯
------------------------------------]	◯	◯	◯
------------------------------------]	◯	◯	◯
------------------------------------]	◯	◯	◯
------------------------------------]	◯	◯	◯
------------------------------------]	◯	◯	◯
------------------------------------]	◯	◯	◯
------------------------------------]	◯	◯	◯
------------------------------------]	◯	◯	◯
------------------------------------]	◯	◯	◯
------------------------------------]	◯	◯	◯

NOTES:

Symptom Log

Description MILD   MOD   SEVERE

--------------------------------------] ◯ ◯ ◯

--------------------------------------] ◯ ◯ ◯

--------------------------------------] ◯ ◯ ◯

--------------------------------------] ◯ ◯ ◯

--------------------------------------] ◯ ◯ ◯

--------------------------------------] ◯ ◯ ◯

--------------------------------------] ◯ ◯ ◯

--------------------------------------] ◯ ◯ ◯

--------------------------------------] ◯ ◯ ◯

--------------------------------------] ◯ ◯ ◯

--------------------------------------] ◯ ◯ ◯

NOTES:

Symptom Log

Description	MILD	MOD	SEVERE
-----------------------------------]	◯	◯	◯
-----------------------------------]	◯	◯	◯
-----------------------------------]	◯	◯	◯
-----------------------------------]	◯	◯	◯
-----------------------------------]	◯	◯	◯
-----------------------------------]	◯	◯	◯
-----------------------------------]	◯	◯	◯
-----------------------------------]	◯	◯	◯
-----------------------------------]	◯	◯	◯
-----------------------------------]	◯	◯	◯
-----------------------------------]	◯	◯	◯

NOTES:

Symptom Log

Description	MILD	MOD	SEVERE
------------------------------------]	◯	◯	◯
------------------------------------]	◯	◯	◯
------------------------------------]	◯	◯	◯
------------------------------------]	◯	◯	◯
------------------------------------]	◯	◯	◯
------------------------------------]	◯	◯	◯
------------------------------------]	◯	◯	◯
------------------------------------]	◯	◯	◯
------------------------------------]	◯	◯	◯
------------------------------------]	◯	◯	◯
------------------------------------]	◯	◯	◯

NOTES:

Symptom Log

Description	MILD	MOD	SEVERE
------------------------------]	◯	◯	◯
------------------------------]	◯	◯	◯
------------------------------]	◯	◯	◯
------------------------------]	◯	◯	◯
------------------------------]	◯	◯	◯
------------------------------]	◯	◯	◯
------------------------------]	◯	◯	◯
------------------------------]	◯	◯	◯
------------------------------]	◯	◯	◯
------------------------------]	◯	◯	◯
------------------------------]	◯	◯	◯

NOTES:

Symptom Log

Description	MILD	MOD	SEVERE
------------------------------------]	◯	◯	◯
------------------------------------]	◯	◯	◯
------------------------------------]	◯	◯	◯
------------------------------------]	◯	◯	◯
------------------------------------]	◯	◯	◯
------------------------------------]	◯	◯	◯
------------------------------------]	◯	◯	◯
------------------------------------]	◯	◯	◯
------------------------------------]	◯	◯	◯
------------------------------------]	◯	◯	◯
------------------------------------]	◯	◯	◯

NOTES:

Symptom Log

Description	MILD	MOD	SEVERE
------------------------------------]	◯	◯	◯
------------------------------------]	◯	◯	◯
------------------------------------]	◯	◯	◯
------------------------------------]	◯	◯	◯
------------------------------------]	◯	◯	◯
------------------------------------]	◯	◯	◯
------------------------------------]	◯	◯	◯
------------------------------------]	◯	◯	◯
------------------------------------]	◯	◯	◯
------------------------------------]	◯	◯	◯
------------------------------------]	◯	◯	◯

NOTES:

Symptom Log

Description	MILD	MOD	SEVERE
------------------------------------]	◯	◯	◯
------------------------------------]	◯	◯	◯
------------------------------------]	◯	◯	◯
------------------------------------]	◯	◯	◯
------------------------------------]	◯	◯	◯
------------------------------------]	◯	◯	◯
------------------------------------]	◯	◯	◯
------------------------------------]	◯	◯	◯
------------------------------------]	◯	◯	◯
------------------------------------]	◯	◯	◯
------------------------------------]	◯	◯	◯

NOTES:

Symptom Log

Description	MILD	MOD	SEVERE
----------------------------------]	◯	◯	◯
----------------------------------]	◯	◯	◯
----------------------------------]	◯	◯	◯
----------------------------------]	◯	◯	◯
----------------------------------]	◯	◯	◯
----------------------------------]	◯	◯	◯
----------------------------------]	◯	◯	◯
----------------------------------]	◯	◯	◯
----------------------------------]	◯	◯	◯
----------------------------------]	◯	◯	◯
----------------------------------]	◯	◯	◯

NOTES:

Symptom Log

Description	MILD	MOD	SEVERE
--]	○	○	○
--]	○	○	○
--]	○	○	○
--]	○	○	○
--]	○	○	○
--]	○	○	○
--]	○	○	○
--]	○	○	○
--]	○	○	○
--]	○	○	○
--]	○	○	○

NOTES:

Symptom Log

Description	MILD	MOD	SEVERE
---------------------------------]	◯	◯	◯
---------------------------------]	◯	◯	◯
---------------------------------]	◯	◯	◯
---------------------------------]	◯	◯	◯
---------------------------------]	◯	◯	◯
---------------------------------]	◯	◯	◯
---------------------------------]	◯	◯	◯
---------------------------------]	◯	◯	◯
---------------------------------]	◯	◯	◯
---------------------------------]	◯	◯	◯
---------------------------------]	◯	◯	◯

NOTES:

Symptom Log

Description   MILD   MOD   SEVERE

------------------------------------] ◯ ◯ ◯

------------------------------------] ◯ ◯ ◯

------------------------------------] ◯ ◯ ◯

------------------------------------] ◯ ◯ ◯

------------------------------------] ◯ ◯ ◯

------------------------------------] ◯ ◯ ◯

------------------------------------] ◯ ◯ ◯

------------------------------------] ◯ ◯ ◯

------------------------------------] ◯ ◯ ◯

------------------------------------] ◯ ◯ ◯

------------------------------------] ◯ ◯ ◯

NOTES:

Symptom Log

Description	MILD	MOD	SEVERE
-----------------------------------]	○	○	○
-----------------------------------]	○	○	○
-----------------------------------]	○	○	○
-----------------------------------]	○	○	○
-----------------------------------]	○	○	○
-----------------------------------]	○	○	○
-----------------------------------]	○	○	○
-----------------------------------]	○	○	○
-----------------------------------]	○	○	○
-----------------------------------]	○	○	○
-----------------------------------]	○	○	○

NOTES:

not so famous. last. words.

I know all to well how each day is a battle. There are so many days that you may wake up and wonder will this be a good day for me or will it be bad. No one really knows how it is unless they are actually going through having an auto-immune disease and the 100s of symptoms associated with each diagnosis. There are so many things you may want to do but find it harder than others, and there are days it takes pure will to get out of bed. As long as you have a breath you have a hope. Each day has it's battles, but that makes you a warrior, doesn't it? Try each day's approach as this warrior going into battle. You have got this, even when it feels like you don't!

-Rochelle Randall

Made in the USA
Coppell, TX
13 February 2022

73518355R10176